A Conversation with Jonathan Edwards

A Conversation with Jonathan Edwards

by

W. Gary Crampton

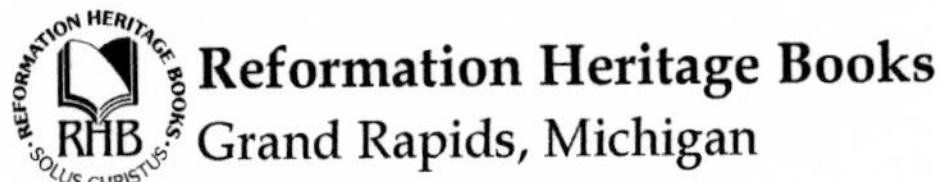

Reformation Heritage Books
Grand Rapids, Michigan

REFORMATION HERITAGE BOOKS
2965 Leonard St., NE
Grand Rapids, MI 49525
616-977-0599 / Fax 616-285-3246
e-mail: orders@heritagebooks.org
website: www.heritagebooks.org

10 digit ISBN #1-892777-76-2
13 digit ISBN #978-1-892777-76-8

Table of Contents

CHAPTER 1
Introduction

Mr. Edwards, first I want to thank you for this series of "conversations" which you have graciously agreed to have with me. It is a privilege as well as a pleasure to be able to discuss some of these matters with you. Without further ado, let's get started.

Do you agree with the Westminster Shorter Catechism *(Q. 1), that man's chief end is to glorify God, and to enjoy Him forever?*

JE: Yes, I do. "It appears that a truly virtuous mind, being as it were under the sovereign dominion of love to God, does above all things seek the glory of God, and makes this his supreme, governing, and ultimate end."[1] "God is the highest good of the reasonable creatures; and the enjoyment of Him is the only happiness with which our souls can be satisfied. To go to heaven, fully to enjoy God, is infinitely better than the most pleasant accommodations here. Fathers and mothers, husbands, wives, or children, or the company of earthly friends, are but shadows; but the enjoyment of God is the substance. These are but scattered beams; but God is the sun. These are but streams; but God is the fountain. These are but drops; but God is the ocean."[2] "Therefore, we are to seek the glory of God as that which is a thing really pleasing to Him."[3]

Since this is the case, is it possible, as some assert, for a converted person to be willing to be damned for the glory of God?

JE: "It is impossible for any [Christian] person to be willing to be perfectly and finally miserable for God's sake, for this supposes love for God is superior to self-love in the most general and extensive sense of self-love, which enters into the nature of love to God.... Love to God, if it be superior to any other principle, will make a man forever unwilling, utterly and finally, to be deprived of that part of his happiness which he has in God's being blessed and glorified, and the more he loves Him, the more unwilling he will be.... The more a man loves God, the more unwilling will he be to be deprived of this happiness."[4] Neither "does any word in the Bible require such self-denial as this."[5]

My grandfather, Solomon Stoddard, taught the same thing. He wrote: "No man acting understandingly is willing to be damned. All ungodly men do interpretatively love damnation (Proverbs 8:35), but no man who understands himself is willing to be damned.... Damnation is a dreadful thing to those who know what it is (Isaiah 33:14).... No such thing is required of men."[6]

If this is the case, what does Paul mean in Romans 9:3 when he says that he could wish himself to be accursed from Christ for the sake of his Jewish kinsmen?

JE: "The apostle's meaning probably is, that he was willing that Christ should so order it that he should in the world be cut off from the society and privileges of His visible people, as an excommunicated person, and also be cut off from the earth by an accursed death at last, dying under the hidings of God's face and dreadful fruits of His displeasure for a time as Christ did."[7]

As you assess your own gifts, how do you think that you can best serve God?

JE: "So far as I myself am able to judge of what talents I have for benefiting my fellow creatures by word, I think I can write better than I can speak."[8]

[1] Edwards, *Works* (Yale), 8:559.
[2] Edwards, *Works*, II:244.
[3] Edwards, *Miscellany* 208.
[4] Edwards, *Miscellany* 530.
[5] Edwards, *Works* (Yale), 4:170.
[6] Solomon Stoddard, *A Guide to Christ*, 53-54.
[7] Cited in Alexander Grosart, *Selections From the Unpublished Writings of Jonathan Edwards*, 154-155.
[8] Edwards, *Works* (Yale), 16:729.

CHAPTER 2

Edwards the Man

I understand that in your youth you had some spiritual experiences which were not truly genuine in nature. Do you think that this is typical? Would you tell us about this?

JE: "I had a variety of concerns and exercises about my soul from my childhood; but I had two more remarkable seasons of awakening before I met with that change by which I was brought to those new dispositions, and the new sense of things, that I have since had. The first time was when I was a boy, some years before I went to college, at a time of remarkable awakening in my father's congregation. I was then very much affected for many months, and concerned about the things of religion, and my soul's salvation; and was abundant in religious duties. I used to pray five times a day in secret, and to spend much time in religious conversation with other boys; and used to meet with them to pray together. I experienced I know not what kind of delight in religion. My mind was much engaged in it, and had much self-righteous pleasure, and it was my delight to abound in religious duties. I, with some of my school-mates, joined together and built a booth in a swamp, in a very retired spot, for a place of prayer. And besides, I had particular secret places of my own in the woods where I used to retire by myself, and was from time to time much affected.... I am ready to think many are deceived with such affections, and such kind of delight as I then had in religion, and mistake it for [saving] grace."[1]

We know that when you were in the Collegiate School at Connecticut (which was later named "Yale"), you studied the Westminster Confession of Faith *along with the* Larger *and* Shorter Catechisms. *Do you agree with this* Confession?

JE: Very much so: "As to my subscribing to the substance of the *Westminster Confession,* there would be no difficulty."[2]

Do you consider yourself to be a Calvinist?

JE: "I should not take it at all amiss, to be called a Calvinist, for distinction's sake; though I utterly disclaim a dependence on Calvin, or believing the doctrines which I hold, because he believed and taught them; and cannot justly be charged of believing everything just as he taught."[3]

Do you have a high view of John Calvin?

JE: Yes, I do. Surely, he "was one of the eminent of the Reformers."[4]

As a Calvinist, do you subscribe to the "Five Points of Calvinism" as set forth in the Synod of Dort (1618-1619)?

JE: I do. As I point out in the "Conclusion" of my *The Freedom of the Will,* "the Calvinistic doctrine of the total depravity and corruption of man's nature," "the doctrine of God's... [unconditional] absolute, eternal, personal election," the doctrine of the "particular design of [Christ's] death [i.e., limited atonement]," the doctrine of "efficacious [irresistible] grace," and the doctrine of the "necessary, infallible perseverance... of the saints," are all biblical truths.[5]

It has been said that from early on you learned to study "with pen in hand," to capture your thoughts on matters you were contemplating.

JE: This is true. "My method of study...has been very

much by writing; applying myself, in this way, to improve every important hint; pursuing the clue to my utmost, when anything in reading, meditation, or conversation, has been suggested to my mind, that seemed to promise light in any weighty point; thus penning what appeared to me my best thoughts, on innumerable subjects, for my own benefit."[6]

Apparently you were genuinely converted in the spring of 1721. According to your own personal account, the doctrine of God's absolute sovereignty, especially in matters of election and reprobation, had previously seemed to you as a "horrible doctrine." Later, however, your thoughts were changed.

JE: Yes, by the grace of God "I seemed to be convinced, and fully satisfied, as to the sovereignty of God, and His justice in thus eternally disposing of men, according to His sovereign pleasure.... However, my mind rested in it; and it put an end to all those cavils and objections. And there has been a wonderful alteration in my mind, with respect to the doctrine of God's sovereignty, from that day to this; so that I scarce ever have found so much as the rising of an objection against it.... I have often since that first conviction, had quite another kind of sense of God's sovereignty than I had then. I have often since had not only a conviction, but a delightful conviction. The doctrine has very often appeared exceedingly pleasant, bright, and sweet. Absolute sovereignty is what I love to ascribe to God."[7]

What is this "new sense" that you speak of?

JE: It mainly consists in a "spiritual understanding...or [a] taste of the moral beauty of divine things." "The immediate object of it [the new sense] is the supreme beauty and excellency of the nature of divine things, as they are in themselves." Therefore, "this spiritual sense is infinitely more noble than...any other principle of discerning that a man naturally has," and "all true experimental knowledge of religion" is derived from it.[8] With this "spiritual understanding," the saints "have a distinguishing taste and relish [of divine things], more and more perfect as they have more holiness."[9] Herein "the sanctifying influence of the Spirit of God rectifies the taste of the soul, whereby it savors those things that are holy and agreeable to God's mind."[10]

Was there a particular verse of Scripture that led you to this "delightful conviction" and a "new sense" of divine things?

JE: "The first instance, that I remember, of that sort of inward, sweet delight in God and divine things, that I have lived much in since, was on reading those words, 1 Timothy 1:17: 'Now unto the King eternal, immortal, invisible, the only wise God, be honor and glory for ever and ever. Amen.' As I read the words, there came into my soul, and was as it were diffused through it, a sense of the glory of the Divine Being; a new sense, quite different from any thing I ever experienced before. Never any words of Scripture seemed to me as these words did. I thought with myself, how excellent a Being that was, and how happy I should be, if I might enjoy that God, and be rapt up to Him in heaven; and be as it were swallowed up in Him forever! I kept saying, and as it were singing, over these words of Scripture to myself; and went to pray to God that I might enjoy Him; and prayed in a manner quite different from what I used to do, with a new sort of affection."[11]

Was there evidence of a genuine conversion, i.e., this "new sense," in your life?

JE: Yes, "After this [conversion] my sense of divine things gradually increased, and became more lively, and more of the inward sweetness. The appearance of everything was altered; there seemed to be, as it were, a calm, sweet cast, or appearance of divine glory, in almost every thing. God's excellency, His wisdom, His purity and love, seemed to appear in every thing.... I was almost always constantly in ejaculatory prayer, wherever I was. Prayer seemed to be natural to me, as the breath by which the inward burnings of my heart had vent. The delights which I now felt in those things of religion, were of an exceeding different kind from those before mentioned, that I had when a boy; and what I then had no more notion of than one born blind has of pleasant and beautiful colors. They were of a more inward, pure, soul-animating and refreshing nature. Those former delights never reached the heart; and did not rise from any sight of the divine excellency of the things of God; or any taste of the soul-satisfying and life-giving good there is in them."[12]

Would you say, then, that without this kind of evidence, there is no reason for a person to believe that he is converted?

JE: Yes, I would. "The Scripture representations of conversion do strongly imply and signify a change of nature.... Therefore if there be no great and remarkable, abiding change in persons, that think they have experienced a work of conversion, vain are all their imaginations and pretenses, however they have been affected. Conversion...is a great and universal change of man, turning him from sin to God. A man may be restrained from sin, before he is converted; but when he is converted, he is not only restrained from sin, his very heart and nature is turned from it, unto holiness; so that thenceforward he becomes a holy person."[13] "Persons after their conversion often speak of things of religion as seeming new to them; that preaching is a new thing; that it seems to them they never heard preaching before; that the Bible is a new book; they find there new chapters, new psalms, new histories, because they see them in a new light."[14]

Is it true that at one time you were very much afraid of thunder storms, but that after your conversion this changed dramatically?

JE: Yes. "Before, I used to be uncommonly terrified with thunder, and to be struck with terror when I saw a thunder-storm rising; but now, on the contrary, it rejoiced me. I felt God, if I may so speak, at the first appearance of a thunder-storm; and used to take the opportunity, at such times, to fix myself in order to view the clouds, and see the lightning play, and hear the majestic and awful voice of God's thunders, which oftentimes was exceedingly entertaining, leading me to sweet contemplations of my great and glorious God."[15]

It is also well known that in your early years you began to write down a series of personal Resolutions. *Could you give us some examples of these?*

JE: Certainly. Resolution #1: "Resolved, that I will do whatsoever I think to be most to the glory of God, and my own good, profit, and pleasure, in the whole of my duration; without any consideration of the time, whether now, or ever so many myriads of ages hence. Resolved, to do whatever I think to be my duty, and most for the good and advantage of mankind in general. Resolved, so to do, whatever difficulties I meet with, how many so ever, and how great so ever." Resolution #4: "Resolved, never to do any manner of thing, whether in soul or body, less or more, than what tends to the glory of God." Resolution #7: "Resolved, never to do any thing, which I should be afraid to do, if it were the last hour of my life." Resolution #28: "Resolved, to study the Scriptures so steadily, constantly, and frequently, as that I may find, and plainly perceive, myself to grow in the knowledge of the same." Resolution #42: "Resolved, frequently to renew the dedication of myself to God, which was made at my baptism; which I solemnly renewed, when I was received into the communion of the church." Resolution #53: "Resolved, to improve every opportunity, when I am in the best and happiest frame of mind, to cast and venture my soul on the Lord Jesus Christ, to trust and confide in Him, and consecrate myself wholly to Him; that from this I may have assurance of my safety, knowing that I confide in my Redeemer." Resolution #69: "Resolved, always to do that, which I shall wish I had done when I see others do it." Resolution #70: "Resolved, let there be something of benevolence, in all that I speak."[16]

I understand that it is when you were twenty and Sarah Pierpont was but thirteen, that you became very impressed with her. Did you see her as that model of Proverbs 31:10-31?

JE: I did. This is what I wrote about her at that time. "They say there is a young lady in New Haven who is beloved of that Great Being [the triune God of Scripture] who made and rules the world, and there are certain seasons in which this Great Being, in some way or other invisible, comes to her and fills her mind with exceeding sweet delight, and that she hardly cares for any thing, except to meditate on Him—that she expects after a while to be received up where He is, to be raised up out of the world and caught up into heaven; being assured that He loves her too well to let her remain at a distance from Him always. There she is to dwell with Him, and to be ravished with His love and delight for ever. Therefore, if you present all the world before her, with the richest of its treasures, she disregards it and cares not for it, and is unmindful of any pain or affliction. She has a strange sweetness in her mind, and singular purity in her affections; is most just and conscientious in all her conduct; and you could not persuade her to do anything wrong or sinful, if you would give her all the world, lest she should offend this Great Being. She is of a wonderful sweetness, calmness and universal benevolence of mind; especially after this great God has manifested Himself to her mind. She will sometimes go about from place to place, singing sweetly; and she seems to be always full of joy and pleasure; and no one knows for what. She loves to be alone, walking in the fields and groves, and seems to have some one invisible always conversing with her."[17]

Here you are talking about Sarah and her love for God. Apparently one way that this is manifest is in her prayer life. Tell us about the importance of prayer in the Christian life.

JE: "A holy life is a life of faith. The life that true Christians live in the world, they live by the faith of the Son of God. But who can believe that that man lives by faith who lives without prayer, which is the natural expression of faith? Prayer is as natural an expression of faith as breathing is of life; and to say that a man lives by faith and lives a prayerless life is every whit as inconsistent and incredible as to say that a man lives without breathing. A prayerless life is so far from being a holy life that it is a profane life."[18] Further, "a true Christian doubtless delights in religious fellowship and Christian conversation, and finds much to affect his heart in it, but he also delights at times to retire from all mankind to converse with God.... True religion disposes persons to be much alone in solitary places for holy meditation and prayer. So it wrought in Isaac (Genesis 24:63). And which is much more, so it wrought in Jesus Christ. How often do we read of His retiring into mountains and solitary places, for holy converse with the Father.... The most eminent divine favors which the saints obtained, that we read of in Scripture, were in their retirement.... [I]t is the nature of true grace...to delight in retirement, and secret converse with God."[19]

I understand that it has been your practice to rise at four or five in the morning to start your day with prayer and Bible study. Does this scheduling have biblical warrant?

JE: Yes, "I think Christ has recommended rising early in the morning, by His rising from the grave very early."[20] From early on in my own ministry "I spent most of my time in thinking of divine things, year after year; often walking alone in the woods, and solitary places, for meditation, soliloquy, and prayer, and converse with God; and it was always my manner, at such times, to sing forth my contemplations. I was almost constantly in ejaculatory prayer, wherever I was. Prayer seemed to be natural to me, as the breath by which the inward burnings of my heart had vent."[21]

What about the person who claims to be a Christian, yet is deficient in prayer?

JE: "I would exhort those who have entertained a hope of being true converts, and yet since their supposed conversion have left off the duty of secret prayer and ordinarily allow themselves in the omission of it, to throw away their hope. If you have left off calling upon God, it is time for you to leave off hoping and flattering yourselves with an imagination that you are the children of God."[22]

Is the non-believer able to truly pray and praise God?

JE: No, "if you have not a work of conversion wrought in you, you will do nothing to any purpose in this work of praise. An unconverted person never once sincerely or acceptably praises God."[23]

Does God ever answer the prayers of non-believers?

JE: Yes, "God is pleased sometimes to answer the prayers of unbelievers. Indeed, He does not hear their prayers for their goodness or acceptableness, or because of any true respect to Him manifested in them, for there is none. Nor has He obliged Himself to answer such prayers. Yet He is pleased sometimes, of His sovereign mercy, to pity wicked men and hear their cries. Thus He heard the cries of the Ninevites (Jonah 3) and the prayer of Ahab (1 Kings 21:27-28)."[24] "Our prayers are loathsome [to God] till they are presented by Him [Christ] in His intercession."[25]

Certainly this would mean that the father, as the head of his family, should continue to be concerned for the spiritual state of his family. Is this a continual requirement for the father?

JE: I believe so. As late as 1753, I wrote to my sickly, married daughter Esther Edwards Burr as follows: "I would not have you think that any strange thing has happened to you in this affliction: it is according to the course of things in this world, that after the world's smiles, some great affliction soon comes. God has now given you early and seasonable warning, not at all to depend on worldly prosperity. Therefore I would advise, if it pleases God to restore you, to let upon no happiness here. Labor while you live, to serve God and do what good you can, and endeavor to improve every dispensation to God's glory and your own spiritual good, and be content to do and bear all that God calls you to in this wilderness, and never expect to find this world anything better than a wilderness. Lay your account to travel through it in weariness, painfulness and trouble, and wait for your rest and your prosperity till hereafter, where they that die in the Lord rest from their labors, and enter into the joy of the Lord. You are like to spend the rest of your life (if you should get over this illness) at a great distance from your parents; but care not much for that. If you lived near us, yet our breath and yours would soon go forth, and we should return to our dust, whither we are all hastening. It is of infinitely more importance to have the presence of an heavenly Father, and to make progress towards an heavenly home. Let us take care that we may meet there at last."[26]

Some persons have accused you of preaching a "scare theology." How do you respond to this?

JE: "Scripture warnings [are] best adapted to the conversion of sinners."[27] Particularly, "the consideration of hell commonly is the first thing that rouses sleeping sinners. By this means their sins are set before them."[28] "If there be really a hell of such dreadful, and never-ending torments, as is generally supposed, that multitudes are in great danger of, and that the bigger part of men in Christian countries do actually from generation to generation fall into, for want of a sense of the terribleness of it, and their danger of it, and so for want of taking due care to avoid it; then why is it not proper for those that have the care of souls, to take great pains to make men sensible of it? Why should they not be told as much of the truth as can be? If I am in danger of going to hell, I should be glad to know as much as possibly I can of the dreadfulness of it.... Some talk of it as an unreasonable thing to frighten persons into heaven; but I think it is a reasonable thing to endeavor to frighten persons away from hell that stand on the brink of it, and are just ready to fall into it, and are senseless of their danger."[29]

We need, then, to preach on this subject and focus on the absolute sovereignty of God in salvation.

JE: "I think I have found that no discourses have been more remarkably blessed, than those in which the doctrine of God's absolute sovereignty with regard to the salvation of sinners, and His just liberty with regard to answering the prayers, or succeeding [answering] the pains of natural men, continuing such, have been insisted on. I never found so much immediate saving fruit, in any measure, or any discourses I have offered to my congregation, as some from those words, Romans 3:19, 'That every mouth may be stopped,'[30] endeavoring to show from thence that it would be just with God forever to reject and cast off mere natural men."[31]

There are a number of persons in the alleged Christian camp who seem to be overly occupied with the work of the Holy Spirit, stressing the Spirit without a view to Christ. How would you comment on this?

JE: "The person to whom the Spirit gives testimony and for whom He raises their esteem must be Jesus—the one who appeared in the flesh. No other Christ can stand in His place. No mystical, fantasy Christ! No light within—as the spirit of Quakers extols—can diminish esteem of and dependence upon the outward Christ. The Spirit who gives testimony for this historical Jesus and leads to Him can be no other than the Spirit of God."[32]

Did you see frenetic excesses set in during the Great Awakening?

JE: Yes, "an intemperate, imprudent zeal, and a degree of

enthusiasm [frenetic religious fervor], soon crept in and mingled itself with that revival of religion; and so great and general an awakening being quite a new thing in the land, at least as to all the living inhabitants of it, neither the people nor ministers had learned thoroughly to distinguish between solid religion and its delusive counterfeits."[33]

Zeal, however, can also be a good thing.

JE: Yes, it can. I believe that "there is nothing that belongs to Christian experience that is more liable to a corrupt mixture than zeal; though it [zeal] be an excellent virtue, a heavenly flame, when it is pure."[34]

The enthusiasts also tend to see the work of the Spirit as separate from the Word of God, do they not?

JE: This is very true. Sadly, "we see it common in enthusiasts who oppose Christ that they deprecate this written rule [the Bible] and set up the light within their souls or some other rule above it.... God has given us the sure Word of prophecy as a light shining in a dark place. They who leave that Word to follow such [frenetic] impressions and impulses leave the guidance of the polar star to follow a man with a lamp. No wonder, therefore, that sometimes they are led into woeful extravagances."[35]

---

[1] Edwards, *Works*, I:xii.

[2] Edwards, *Works*, I:cxxi.

[3] Edwards, *Works* (Yale), 1:131.

[4] Edwards, *Works* (Yale), 9:422.

[5] Edwards, *The Freedom of the Will*, 322ff. The "Five Points of Calvinism" are expressed in the acrostic TULIP: total depravity, unconditional election, limited atonement, irresistible grace, and the perseverance of the saints.

[6] Edwards, *Works*, I:clxxiv.

[7] Edwards, *Works*, I:xii-xiii.

[8] Edwards, *Works* (Yale), 2:273, 271, 275.

[9] Edwards, *Miscellany* 141.

[10] Edwards, *Works* (Yale), 4:437.

[11] Edwards, *Works*, I:xiii.

[12] Edwards, *Works*, I:xiii.
[13] Edwards, *Works* (Yale), 2:340-341.
[14] Edwards, *Works* (Yale), 4:181.
[15] Edwards, *Works*, I:xiii.
[16] Edwards, *Works* (Yale), 16:753-759. There were seventy Resolutions in all.
[17] Cited in Ian Murray, *Jonathan Edwards: A New Biography*, 92.
[18] Edwards, *Sermon* on Job 27:10.
[19] Edwards, *Works*, I:311-312.
[20] Cited in George M. Marsden, *Jonathan Edwards: A Life*, 133.
[21] Jonathan Edwards, *Jonathan Edwards: Representative Selections*, 61.
[22] Edwards, *Sermon* on Job 27:10.
[23] Edwards, *Sermon* on Revelation 14:2.
[24] Edwards, *Sermon* on Psalm 65:2.
[25] Edwards, *Sermon* on Hebrews 9:12.
[26] Edwards, *A Jonathan Edwards Reader*, 312.
[27] Edwards, *Sermon* on Luke 16:31.
[28] Edwards, *Sermon* on Hebrews 9:12.
[29] Edwards, *Works* (Yale), 4:246-248.
[30] This was Edwards' text for his sermon "The Justice of God in the Damnation of Sinners."
[31] Edwards, *Works* (Yale), 4:168.
[32] Cited in Archie Parrish and R. C. Sproul, *The Spirit of Revival*, 30.
[33] Edwards, *Works*, II:321.
[34] Edwards, *Works* (Yale), 4:460.
[35] Cited in Parrish and Sproul, *The Spirit of Revival*, 33, 136.

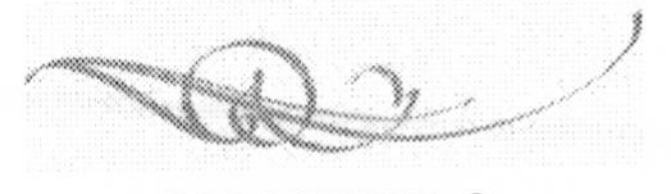

CHAPTER 3
Edwards on Knowledge

According to John Calvin, without a knowledge of one's self, there is no knowledge of God. But to know one's self, God's image bearer, there must first be a knowledge of God. God, then, must be the first object of knowledge. Is this your thought as well?

JE: Yes, it is. "Of all kinds of knowledge that we can ever obtain, the knowledge of God, and the knowledge of ourselves, are the most important. As [the Christian] religion is the great business for which we are created, and on which our happiness depends; and as [the Christian] religion consists in an intercourse between ourselves and our Maker; and so has its foundation in God's nature and ours, and in the relation that God and we stand in to each other; therefore, a true knowledge of both must be necessary, in order to true religion."[1] "The more he [man] knows of God the more he will know of himself.... Indeed, he who does not have the true knowledge of God has no true knowledge of anything."[2]

How does one come to this knowledge of God and self?

JE: Only by means of Scripture. Scripture gives us the knowledge which "is the key that first opens the hard heart and enlarges the affections, and so opens the way for men into the kingdom of heaven."[3] "The doctrines of the Word of God are the foundation of all useful and excellent knowledge."[4] If men "are not led by [special] revelation and direct teaching into a right way of using their reason, in arguing from effects to causes, etc., they would forever remain in the most woeful doubt, and uncertainty concerning the nature and the very being of God."[5]

As you know, the principle of sola Scriptura, *that the Bible alone is the Word of God, and that it has a monopoly on truth, is taught in the* Westminster Confession of Faith *(1:6) as follows: "The whole counsel of God concerning all things necessary for His own glory, man's salvation, faith, and life, is either expressly set down in Scripture, or by good and necessary consequence may be deduced from Scripture: unto which nothing at any time is to be added, whether by new revelations of the Spirit, or traditions of men." Do you agree with this teaching?*

JE: I most assuredly do. "Where is [there] any Word of God if it be not in the Bible?"[6] "The doctrines of the Word of God are the foundation of all useful and excellent knowledge."[7] "God would have our whole dependence be upon the Scriptures because the greater our dependence is on the Word of God, the more direct and immediate is our dependence on God Himself."[8] "God has given us His Word to this very end that it might be our rule.... And strictly speaking, this is our only rule. If we join anything else to it, as making it our rule, we do that which we have no warrant for, yes that which God has forbidden. See Deuteronomy 4:2; Proverbs 30:6."[9]

It is also noteworthy that this teaching of the Westminster Assembly maintains that the truth of Scripture is not restricted to the explicit statements of the Bible. Those things which can be logically deduced "by good and necessary consequence" are also God's truth. Is this also your view?

JE: Yes, "if what the Scripture says, together with what is plain to reason, leads [us] to believe any doctrine, we are to look upon ourselves as taught this doctrine from Scripture. God may reveal things in Scripture, which way He pleases; if by what He there reveals the thing is in any way clearly discovered to the understanding or eye of the mind, it is our duty to receive it as His revelation."[10]

As you know, many persons with an Enlightenment mentality assert that reason takes precedence over special revelation. I am quite confident that even with your high view of reason (i.e., logic) you are opposed to this Enlightenment thinking.

JE: Yes, I am. "That rule of interpreting Scripture so much insisted upon by many of late, *viz.* first to determine by our reason what is agreeable to the moral perfections of God and then to interpret the Scriptures by them, is an unjust and fallacious one...the infinitely great and wise Sovereign of heaven and earth [does not] wait for the decision of judgment and reason what laws or rules of proceeding in Him are just in order to require our submission to Him."[11]

At the same time, you are saying that sound reasoning, i.e., logic, is imperative for the sound interpretation of Scripture.

JE: That's correct. Scripture is the source of truth. But "there is perfect harmony" between reason and biblical revelation.[12] There "is the most sweet harmony between Christianity and reason."[13] There is an "agreeableness of the Christian religion to reason."[14] Christian man, then, is to reason from Scripture, not to it. "Revelation is given as a rule to reason."[15]

Now we know that you are an empiricist, believing that the source of all knowledge is to be found in experience.

JE: I am. "All ideas begin from [sensation], and there can never be any idea, thought or act of the mind unless the mind first received some ideas from sensation, or some other way equivalent, wherein the mind is wholly passive in receiving them."[16]

But even here your views of empiricism differ greatly from other empiricists, because you do not believe that sensation can produce any knowledge.

JE: This is true. It is God who "immediately" produces knowledge in the mind of all who receive knowledge. "Thus the matter is as to the Holy Spirit's gracious operations on the mind. We have shown in philosophy that all natural operations are done immediately by God only in harmony and proportion."[17] And when it comes to the divine light or the grace of salvific knowledge, here "there is such a thing as a spiritual and divine light, immediately imparted to the soul by God, of a different nature from any that is obtained by natural causes" (such as sensation).[18]

I assume that you would say, then, that it is the Word of God and not experience that is to be our guide.

JE: Indeed, I would. "Scripture is the highest rule." Scripture "is [always] a more sure guide…than experience."[19]

It is your view that Holy Scripture is the rule of judging all matters of the Christian faith, and not philosophical arguments?

JE: Correct. "The light of nature is in no sense whatsoever sufficient to discover this [Christian] religion."[20] Apart from special revelation, "the very notion of such a Being [God] is all mystery, involving nothing but incomprehensible paradoxes, and seeming inconsistencies."[21] In fact, "were it not for divine [special] revelation, I am persuaded, that there is not one doctrine of that which we call natural religion, which, not withstanding all philosophy and learning, would not be forever involved in darkness, doubts, endless disputes, and dreadful confusion."[22]

You are of the belief, as we understand it, that there is no true knowledge of God apart from Scripture.

JE: Absolutely so. "Now there is nothing else that informs us what this scheme and design of God in His works is but only the holy Scriptures. Nothing else pretends to set in view the whole series of God's works of providence from beginning to end, and to show how all things were from God at first, and what end they are for, and how they are ordered from the beginning, and how they will proceed to the end of the world, and what they will come to at last, and how then all things shall be to God. Nothing else but the Scriptures has any pretense for showing any manner of regular scheme or drift in those revolutions which God orders from age to age. Nothing else pretends to show what God would by the things that He has done and is doing and will do, what He seeks and intends by them. Nothing else pretends to show with any distinctness or certainty how the world began at first, or to tell us the original of things. Nothing but the Scriptures sets forth how God has governed the world from the beginning of the generations of men on the earth in an orderly history, and nothing else sets before us how He will govern it to the end by an orderly prophecy of future events, agreeable to the challenge that God makes to the gods and prophets and teachers of the heathen in Isaiah 41:22-23: 'Let them bring forth, and show us what shall happen; let them show the former things, what they be, that we may consider them, and know the latter end of them; or declare us things to come. Show the things that are to come hereafter, that we may know that you are gods.'"[23]

As you very well know, throughout the history of philosophic inquiry there have been a number of philosophers who hold to a form of "idealism," i.e., that the objects of knowledge are considered to be completely dependent on the mind of man. The only things which exist are those things which are known. What are your thoughts here?

JE: I am an idealist. I will explain it this way: "We know there was being from eternity; and this being must be intelligent, for how could our mind refuse to believe that there should be being from all eternity without its being conscious to itself that it was. That there should be something from all eternity, and yet not know all that while that anything is, is really a contradiction. We may see it to be so though we do not know how to express it. For in what respect does anything have being when it is not conscious of its own being? And in what respect does anything have a being that neither angels nor men nor any other created intelligence know nothing of, but only as God knows it to be? Not at all, any more than there are sounds where none hears or colors where none sees. Thus, for instance, suppose that there is a room in which no one is; no one sees in that room, there is no created intelligence. The things in the room have no being in any other way than as God is conscious of them, for there is no color, nor any sound, nor any shape.... For we are to remember that the world exists only mentally, so that the very being of the world implies it being perceived or discovered."[24] Now when "I say that the material universe exists only in the mind, I mean that it is absolutely dependent on the conception of the mind for its existence, and does not exist as spirits do, whose existence does not consist in, nor in dependence upon, the conception of other minds." The "existence of the whole material universe is absolutely dependent on idea."[25]

Does this mean that all truth exists in the mind of God, and that no truth exists outside of God's mind?

JE: Yes, it does. "All truth is in the mind...[and] God is truth itself," so if we are going to know the truth there must be "the consistency and agreement of our ideas with the ideas of God."[26]

If this is so, then would you say that God has created human beings (His image bearers) with rational minds that use the same laws of thought as His own, so that the principles of reason (logic) and knowledge are innately given by God to mankind?

JE: Yes, I would say this. The rules of logic, our "reasoning," is an "innate principle," i.e., "the soul is born with it."[27]

But you also hold to the doctrine of occasionalism, i.e., that God is the efficient cause of all things, whereby with every "occasion" of the consent of the mind of man to act in a certain way, God moves to bring about that act; the movement of the creature is only the "occasion" in which God acts.

JE: Yes, I do: "Indeed, in natural things means of effects, in metaphysical strictness, are not proper cause of the effects, but only occasions. God produces all effects, but yet He ties natural events to the operation of such means, or causes them to be consequent on such means according to fixed, determinate and unchangeable rules, which are called the laws of nature."[28]

General and Special Revelation

Theologians tell us that the triune God has revealed Himself to man in both general and special revelation, which are in harmony. The former, we are told, is general in audience (all mankind) and limited in content, whereas the latter, which is now found in Scripture alone, is more restricted in audience (those who read the Bible), and much more detailed in content. Moreover, due to its limited nature, general revelation must always be interpreted in light of special revelation. Is this your view?

JE: Yes, it is. "As the system of nature and the system of [special] revelation are both divine works, so both are in different senses a divine word, both are the voice of God to intelligent creatures, a manifestation and declaration of Himself to mankind."[29] "The works [general revelation] of God are but a kind of voice or language of God to instruct intelligent beings in things pertaining to Himself"; and these works "confirm the Scriptures, for an excellent agreement exists between these things and the holy Scriptures."[30] Moreover, "the book of Scripture is the interpreter of the book of nature."[31]

Psalm 19 speaks of the fact that the universe itself reveals the majesty of God.

JE: Correct. "I am not ashamed to own that I believe that

the whole universe, heaven and earth, air and seas...be full of images of divine things, as full as a language is of words."[32] "The whole creation of God preaches...[and the] providence of God preaches aloud."[33] "The beauty of the world is a communication of God's beauty."[34]

Do you believe that in general revelation God has implanted an innate knowledge of Himself in all men (to include the moral law of God), which is propositional and ineradicable?

JE: I do indeed.[35] "Things that we know by immediate sensation, we know intuitively, and they are properly self-evident [innate] truths." "We know our own existence, and the existence of everything that we are conscious of in our own minds, intuitively." For example, "when we...see anything begin to be, we intuitively know there is a cause.... This is an innate principle...that the soul is born with."[36]

Is this the same thing as the "conscience" of man?

JE: Yes, "natural conscience...concurs with the law of God, and is of equal extent with it, and joins its voice with it in every article."[37]

Do you agree that the propositional special revelation of Scripture is necessary for man to come to a sound and saving knowledge of God?

JE: Yes, this is correct. "The light of nature teaches that religion which is necessary to continue in the favor of God that made us, but it cannot teach us that religion which is necessary to our being restored to the favor of God, after we have forfeited it."[38] "I am of the mind that mankind would have been like a parcel of beasts with respect to their knowledge in all important truths, if there had never been any such thing as [special] revelation in the world."[39] "It is the gospel, and that only, that has actually been the means to bring the world to the knowledge of the true God."[40]

Are you in full agreement with the Westminster Assembly and Reformed theology in general that special revelation is necessary due to the inadequacy of general revelation?

JE: I am. It is due to this inadequacy that it "plainly appears the necessity of divine [special] revelation."[41] "There are many truths concerning God, and our duty to Him, which are evident by the light of nature." But "Christian divinity…is not evident by the light of nature; it depends on [special] revelation…. It is only the Word of God, contained in the Old and New Testaments, which teaches us Christian divinity." Scripture "is the fountain whence all knowledge in divinity must be derived."[42]

Do you believe that Scripture is the sole source of truth to which we have access this side of the final state?

JE: I do. "Revelation is that light in the world from whence has beamed forth not only the knowledge of religion, but all valuable truth."[43]

Do you believe, as Calvin taught, that the Scriptures are self-authenticating?

JE: Yes, I agree that "the Scriptures themselves are an evidence of their own divine authority."[44] "It surely becomes us to receive what God reveals to be true, and to look upon His Word as proof sufficient, whether what He reveals squares with our notions or not."[45] The Word of God does not "go about begging for its evidence, so much as some think; it has its highest and most proper evidence in itself."[46] The Scriptures "prove themselves by their own powerful light to be of divine authority."[47] "God may reveal things in Scripture…it is our duty to receive it as His revelation," simply because it is the Word of God.[48]

You do not deny, do you, that there are a number of evidences that the Bible is the Word of God?

JE: Not at all. God's Word is "a transcript of the divine

perfections."[49] "There are signatures of divine majesty to be seen in the Word, and signatures of divine wisdom and of divine holiness, and the evident marks of divine grace, that make it evident that the Word of God did proceed from a divine majesty and wisdom and holiness and grace."[50] Also, "the admirable consent and agreement" regarding the biblical teaching on the coming of Christ "is, therefore, a clear and certain evidence of the divine authority of these writings."[51]

And could we not use these evidences in the area of apologetics?

JE: Of course we should. Even though Scripture is self-evidencing and self-authenticating, still "great use may be made of external arguments, [and] they are not to be neglected, but highly prized and valued; for they may be greatly serviceable to awaken unbelievers, and bring them to serious consideration, and to confirm the faith of true saints."[52] But apart from the inner testimony of the Holy Spirit these evidences are vain. They "cannot be sufficient.... It is impossible that men...should come at the force of arguments for the truth of Christianity."[53]

Yet, the evidences do not prove the Bible to be the Word of God.

JE: Correct. If men "are not led by [special] revelation and direct teaching into a right way of using their reason, in arguing from effects to causes, etc., they would forever remain in the most woeful doubt, and uncertainty concerning the nature and the very being of God."[54]

One of the ways you use this kind of evidence in refuting the opponent of the Christian faith is your own form of the ontological argument.

JE: I suppose it could be called that. The argument goes as follows: "That there should be absolutely nothing at all is utterly impossible.... And if any man thinks that he can think well enough how there should be nothing, I'll engage that what he means by 'nothing' is as much something as anything thought of in his life; and I believe that if he knew what nothing really was it would be intuitively evident to him that it could not be. So that we see it is necessary some being should eternally be. And it is a more palpable contradiction still to say that there must be being somewhere, and not elsewhere; for the words 'absolutely nothing' and 'where' contradict each other. And besides, it gives as great a shock to the mind to think of pure nothing in any one place, as it does to think of it in all. So that we see this necessary, eternal being must be infinite and omnipresent."[55]

---

[1] Edwards, *Works,* I:4.

[2] Edwards, *Sermon* on Isaiah 6:5.

[3] Edwards, *Works* (Yale), 2:266.

[4] Edwards, *Miscellany* 350.

[5] Edwards, *Miscellany* 1297.

[6] Edwards, *Sermon* on 2 Timothy 3:16.

[7] Edwards, *Miscellany* 350.

[8] Edwards, *Miscellany* 535.

[9] Edwards, *Works* (Yale), 12:319.

[10] Edwards, *Miscellany* 426.

[11] Edwards, *Sermon* on 1 Corinthians 2:11-13.

[12] Edwards, *Sermon* on Romans 3:11.

[13] Edwards, *Works* (Yale), 8:286-287.

[14] Edwards, *Miscellany* 1156.

[15] Edwards, *Miscellany* 1340.

[16] Edwards, *Works* (Yale), 6:390.

[17] Edwards, *Miscellany* 64.

[18] Edwards, *Sermon* on Matthew 16:17.

[19] Edwards, *Works* (Yale), 21:505.

[20] Edwards, *Miscellany* 1337.

[21] Edwards, *Works,* II:483.

[22] Edwards, *Works,* II:462.

[23] Edwards, *Works* (Yale), 9:520-521.

[24] Cited in *Our Great and Glorious God,* compiled and edited by Don Kistler, 1, 94.

[25] Edwards, *Works* (Yale), 6:368, 353.

[26] Edwards, *Works* (Yale), 6:340-342.

[27] Edwards, *Works* (Yale), 6:370.

[28] Edwards, *Miscellany* 629.

[29] Edwards, *Miscellany* 1340.

[30] Cited in William J. Scheick, *The Writings of Jonathan Edwards,* 5.

[31] Edwards, *Works* (Yale), 11:106.
[32] Edwards, *Works* (Yale), 11:152.
[33] Edwards, *Sermon* on Psalm 95:7-8.
[34] Edwards, *Miscellany* 293.
[35] Edwards, *Miscellany* 119.
[36] Edwards, *Works* (Yale), 6:346, 370.
[37] Edwards, *Works* (Yale), 8:594.
[38] Edwards, *Works*, II:491.
[39] Edwards, *Miscellany* 350.
[40] Edwards, *Works* (Yale), 9:398.
[41] Edwards, *Works* II:253.
[42] Edwards, *Works* II:158, 162.
[43] Edwards, *Miscellany* 350.
[44] Edwards, *Miscellany* 333.
[45] Edwards, *Miscellany* 583.
[46] Edwards, *Works*, I:293.
[47] Edwards, *Sermon* on Psalm 19:7-10.
[48] Edwards, *Miscellany* 426.
[49] Edwards, *Miscellany* 94.
[50] Edwards, *Sermon* on Matthew 13:23.
[51] Cited in Stephen J. Nichols, *An Absolute Sort of Certainty*, 43.
[52] Edwards, *Works*, I:293.
[53] Edwards, *Works*, I:292.
[54] Edwards, *Miscellany* 1297.
[55] Edwards, *Works* (Yale), 6:202.

CHAPTER 4

Edwards on Scripture

I know that you have a very high view of Scripture, and that you have devoted your life to the study of Scripture.

JE: Early on I resolved "To study the Scriptures so steadily, constantly, and frequently, as that I may find, and plainly perceive, myself to grow in the knowledge of the same."[1]

According to the Westminster Shorter Catechism *(Q. 3), "the Scriptures principally teach what man is to believe concerning God, and what duty God requires of man." Is this an accurate statement?*

JE: I believe so. I would say that "we must remember that it [Scripture] is a revelation of what God knows to be the very truth concerning His own nature: of the acts and operations of His mind with respect to His creatures; of the grand scheme of infinite wisdom in His works, especially with respect to the intelligent and moral world; a revelation of the spiritual and visible world; a revelation of that invisible world which men shall belong to after this life; a revelation of the greatest works of God, the manner of His creating the world, and of His governing of it, especially with regard to the higher and more important parts of it.... If God gives a revelation of religious things, it must be mainly concerning the affairs of the moral and intelligent universe: which is the grand system of spirits: it must be chiefly about Himself and intelligent creatures."[2]

Progressive Revelation

Reformed theologians throughout the centuries have held that biblical revelation was progressive in nature; that is, that God has chosen to give us a continuously enlarging body of infallible special revelation from the time of Adam in the Garden of Eden to the time of the apostles. In Eden, God revealed Himself to Adam in propositional revelation, and He continued to do so until the close of the canon of Scripture.

JE: This is my view, as pointed out in my thirty sermon-lectures titled *A History of the Work of Redemption.*[3]

Yes, I have read this magnificent treatise. And in this work you point out that one of the predominant ways that the progress of special revelation is recognizable in the Bible is in the various covenants that God has established with His church, both in the Old and New Testaments.

JE: That is correct. There is a unity that exists between the Old and the New Testaments, a unity which is founded upon the covenant of grace. "The work of redemption is a work that God carries on from the fall of man to the end of the world."[4] There is "the unity of [redemptive] history," wherein we also see the unity of the Word of God.[5] We also see this in that when Christ came, He "did not give to the world any new moral precepts that were not either expressed or implied in the precepts of the Old Testament and in the Ten Commandments."[6]

In chapter 7 ("Of God's Covenant with Man") of the Westminster Confession of Faith, *we read about the covenant of grace. Are you, as a covenant theologian, in basic agreement with this chapter?*

JE: Yes, I am. The covenant of grace is "Christ's last will and testament."[7] And herein "God has become bound to us [the elect] by covenant.... He bound Himself by His Word, His promise...He has bound Himself by His oath."[8]

How important is it for us to understand the nature of covenant theology?

JE: Extremely important, because "God's righteousness, or covenant mercy, is the root, of which His salvation is the fruit.... For salvation is the sum of all those works of God by which the benefits that are by the covenant of grace are procured and bestowed."[9] "God makes no promises of any future eternal good to fallen man in any other covenant but the covenant of grace."[10]

As taught in the Confession *(7:2), prior to this covenant, however, there was a covenant of works established with Adam: "The first covenant made with man was a covenant of works, wherein life was promised to Adam, and in him [as the federal head or representative of the entire human race] to his posterity, upon perfect and personal obedience."*

JE: The Westminster divines are correct. "Perfect obedience is the condition of the first covenant [of works]."[11] And "if Adam our first surety had fulfilled the covenant [of works] made with him...then his posterity...would all have had the title to eternal life by virtue of the promises made to Adam their surety."[12] That is, "Our first surety, if he had stood, would have been brought to eat of the tree of life as a seal of a confirmed state of life in persevering and everlasting holiness and happiness; and he would have eaten of this tree of life as a seal of persevering confirmed life, not only for himself, but as our head. As when he ate of the tree of knowledge of good and evil, he tasted as our head, and so brought death on himself and all his posterity: so if he had persevered, and had eaten of the tree of life, he would have tasted of that as our head, and therein confirmed holiness and life would have been sealed to him and all his posterity."[13] However, "the first covenant failed of bringing men to the glory of God, through man's instability, whereby he failed of perseverance."[14]

We will discuss this further below, but for now, do you believe that the sin of Adam was imputed to his posterity?

JE: I do. "The imputation of Adam's one transgression, is indeed most directly and frequently asserted [in Scripture]."[15]

Why is it that only the first sin of Adam was imputed to his posterity?

JE: Because "the time of Adam's trial as the covenant head of his posterity was over as soon as that act was completed."[16]

What all exactly did Adam break when he sinned in the Garden?

JE: I agree here with Thomas Boston, that "our first parents, by eating the forbidden fruit, 'broke all the ten commands at once.'"[17]

Do you mean that Adam had a knowledge of the ten commandments in the Garden?

JE: "Indeed, the world had their rule of obedience from Adam to Moses, not merely by the light of nature, as it was in them, but had it partly by tradition from Adam, which they might have well delivered for a time, by reason of the long lives of Adam and the other patriarchs; and one reason why God gave express revelation of the law, about Moses' time, seems to have been that then the world began to be at such a remove from Adam, that the light they had by tradition from him began to grow obscure, and to be wore out; but this confirms that Adam had it himself with great clearness."[18]

As a side note, why do you think God cursed the serpent to crawl on his belly?

JE: "This to me looks as a plausible reason, why such a sort of curse was denounced to the serpent as going on his belly. The serpent, in the exercise of his subtlety and craft, used to hide his head and clap down upon his belly. In this temptation he had remarkably exercised that sort of craft and hid himself; therefore he should go after this manner forever after."[19]

Was the covenant of works, as suggested by the Confession *(7:1-2), graciously given by God?*

JE: Indeed, it was. "It was an act of God's goodness and condescension toward man to enter into any covenant at all with him and that He should become engaged to give eternal life to him upon his perfect obedience."[20]

Is this covenant still in force?

JE: I agree here with Thomas Ridgley, that "the obligation thereof, as a law, distinct from a covenant, and the curse, arising from the sanction thereof, remains still in force against fallen man; yet, as a covenant, in which life was promised on condition of obedience, it was from that time, abrogated."[21]

But then, immediately subsequent to the Fall, God entered into a new covenant with His elect: the covenant of grace.

JE: Yes. "God had made a second covenant [of grace] in mercy to fallen man, that in the way of this covenant he might be brought to the glory of God, which he failed of under the other.... Therefore God introduces another better covenant, committed not to his [Adam's] strength, but to the strength of one that was mighty and stable [Christ], and therefore is a sure and everlasting covenant.... The first was only to make way for the second."[22]

With whom was this covenant made?

JE: "God makes the covenant [of grace] with Christ, the second Adam, for Himself and all His posterity [the elect]."[23]

When was this covenant first revealed?

JE: This covenant promise "was first revealed on earth in...Genesis 3:15...these words of God in the fifteenth verse of the third chapter of Genesis were the first dawning of the light of the gospel after this darkness."[24] This is "the first revelation of the covenant of grace."[25] "In those words of God there was an intimation of another surety to be appointed for man after the first surety failed.... It was an obscure revelation of the gospel." Moreover, "that gospel light which dawned immediately after the Fall of man gradually increases," until consummated in the supreme and final revelation of God to man in the person and work of Jesus Christ.[26]

And who were the first people redeemed by the Christ promised in Genesis 3:15?

JE: "It is probable that Adam and Eve...were the first fruits of Christ's redemption."[27]

You are suggesting that the principle of blood sacrifice is established in this first promise.

JE: Correct. "There were beasts slain...by God's appointment in their [Adam's and Eve's] stead, of which God made them coats of skin [Genesis 3:21]."[28]

Do you see some of this concept in the early sacrifices of Cain and Abel (Genesis 4:3-4)?

JE: I certainly do. "Abel...comes with bloody sacrifices, hereby testifying his faith in the promised great sacrifice [Jesus Christ]. Cain comes with his own righteousness.... He comes without any propitiation, with the fruit of his ground, and produce of his own labors, as though he could add something to the Most High by gifts of his own substance. And therefore he was interested in no atonement."[29]

If these things are so, then the Old Covenant is not substantially different from the New.

JE: First, I would say that "there is perhaps no part of divinity attended with so much intricacy, and wherein orthodox divines so much differ, as the stating the precise agreement and difference between the two dispensations of Moses and of Christ."[30] But I would most assuredly say that the covenant "is not essentially different now from...the Old Testament, and even before the flood; and it always will remain the same."[31] Both Testaments have "the same salvation," the "same Mediator" (Jesus Christ), the same method of justification by faith alone in Christ alone, and the same application of Christ's redemptive cross work by means of the Holy Spirit with the Word of God. The two covenants "differ only in manner and circumstances."[32] "The whole book, both Old Testament and New, is filled up with the gospel, only with this difference, that the Old Testament contains the gospel under a veil, but the New contains it unveiled, so that we may see the glory of the Lord with open face."[33] "For though the covenant of grace indeed was in force before His [Christ's] death, yet it was of force no other wise than by His death."[34]

So there really is only one church throughout the entirety of redemptive history?

JE: Absolutely. "Though the dispensations have been altered, yet the religion that the church has professed has always as to its essentials been the same. The church of God from the beginning has been one society."[35]

You also teach that there are two sides to the covenants: God's side and man's side.

JE: That is correct. "In every covenant there is required the consent of both parties. Consent on man's part to God's covenant is only an acceptance of the covenant proposed by God."[36] In this sense, "all the promises of each of these covenants are conditional. To suppose that there are any promises of the covenant of grace, or any covenant promises, that are not conditional promises, seems an absurdity and contradiction."[37]

But I believe that it is also your view, along with many Reformed theologians, that even prior to the unfolding of the covenant of grace there was another supra-temporal, intra-Trinitarian covenant: the covenant of redemption.

JE: Yes, this covenant, which is the foundation of the covenant of grace, purposed the salvation of elect sinners by the person and work of Jesus Christ, their covenant representative. Herein was an "agreement which the persons of the Trinity came into from eternity as it were by mutual consultation and covenant."[38] And the covenant of grace is the working out of the covenant of redemption.[39] "The eternal covenant that was between the Father and the Son, wherein Christ undertook to stand as Mediator with fallen [elect] man, and was appointed thereto by the Father. In that covenant, all things concerning Christ's execution of His mediatorial office, were agreed between Christ and His Father, and established by them. And this covenant or eternal agreement, is the highest rule that Christ acts by in His office; and it is a rule that He never departs from."[40]

What about the Holy Spirit?

JE: Good question. Let me state it this way: In this covenant agreement, "the Father appoints and provides the Redeemer, and Himself accepts the price and grants the thing purchased; the Son is the Redeemer by offering up of Himself, and is the price; and the Holy Ghost immediately communicates to us the thing purchased by communicating Himself, and He is the thing purchased."[41]

I know that it is debated as to whether or not the Greek word diatheke *means "testament" or "covenant." What is your view?*

JE: I have said that the covenant of grace is "Christ's last will and testament."[42] And I believe that it should be viewed this way; that is, it is a covenant which has at its root the testamentary death of the Mediator, Jesus Christ: "This covenant is called a testament in Scripture and compared to a will that is confirmed by the death of a testator. Now the testator that died was Christ...[so] the covenant of grace was His will and testament to His church...[and] Christ and the church are the parties contracting."[43] The "covenant of grace [is] represented as His testament."[44]

It is also well known that you and other New England pastors believe that there is a national covenant which exists between New England and the covenant God.

JE: This is so. New England is a covenant nation, and "God in a national covenant promises prosperity to external duties."[45] Nevertheless, the nation must be aware that "the prevailing of sin and wickedness does exceedingly tend to bring calamity and misery upon any people."[46] On the other hand, peaceableness "conduces to the temporal prosperity of a people."[47] Both for the individual, and for a nation, "the way of duty is the way of prosperity."[48]

Canonization of Scripture

According to Reformed theology, as taught in chapter 1 of the Westminster Confession of Faith, *the doctrine of progressive revelation maintains that the miraculous or charismatic word-gifts (e.g., tongues, prophecy) ceased at the end of the apostolic age, and the canon of Scripture was closed at that time. Because "those former ways of God's revealing His will unto His people [have] now ceased," special revelation is now found in the 66 books of the Old and New Testaments alone. I assume that you agree with this assessment.*

JE: I do. First we should note that "God took this care with respect to the books of the Old Testament, that no books should be received by the Jewish church and delivered down in the canon of the Old Testament but what was His Word and owned by Christ. We may therefore conclude that He would still take the same care of His church with respect to the New Testament."[49] "The canon of Scripture is completed," and it is "that standing rule that God has given to His church, which the apostle teaches us is surer than a voice from heaven."[50]

Your comments here seem to indicate that you would also adhere to the teaching of the Confession *(1:8), that God has not only given us an inspired Word, but has also "by His singular care and providence kept [this Word] pure in all ages." And if this is so, I assume that you would adopt the Majority or Received or Ecclesiastical Text view of textual criticism, rather than the Eclectic or Critical Text view?*

JE: You are correct on both accounts. "If He [God] has ordered it so in His providence, that such and such books should be put into the New Testament received by His church, and from age to age delivered down as such without any distinguishing properties or circumstances, it is His plain voice to us that we must receive it as His Word."[51] "The same Word has been kept all along; it has not been changed."[52]

As a side note here, what do you think of the Septuagint, i.e., the Greek translation of the Hebrew Old Testament?

JE: "This is the first translation that ever was made of the Scriptures that we have any credible account of. The canon of the Old Testament had been completed by Malachi, but about one hundred and twenty years before, in its original. And hitherto the Scriptures had been locked up from all other nations but the Jews in the Hebrew tongue; that was understood by no other nation but they. But now it was translated into the Greek language which…was a language that was commonly understood by the nations of the world."[53]

What about the charismatic word gifts?

JE: "These gifts are not fruits of the Spirit that were given to be continued to the church throughout all ages. They were continued in the church, or at least were granted from time to time, though not without some considerable intermissions, from the beginning of the world till the close of the canon of the Scriptures was completed."[54]

Where does the New Testament specifically teach about the cessation of the charismatic gifts?

JE: In 1 Corinthians 13:8-13. Paul teaches that these gifts

functioned as "childish things," and "they were adapted for the childish state of the church." They were a partial means of special revelation. And they are now supplanted by the perfect, complete Word of God, wherein we have "a perfect rule of faith and practice."[55] "The extraordinary influences of the Spirit of God imparting immediate revelations to men were designed only for a temporary continuance while the church was in its minority and never were intended to be statedly upheld in the Christian church."[56]

When was the canon closed?

JE: No later than the end of the first century, when the apostle John concluded the writing of the New Testament. "So that the canon of the Scriptures, that great and standing written rule, that was begun about Moses' time, is now completed and settled, and a curse is denounced against him that adds anything to it or diminishes anything from it."[57]

What was the final book written?

JE: "The Book of Revelation," which was written by "the apostle John…to shut up the canon of the New Testament, and of the whole Scripture."[58]

Inspiration

You do believe, then, that the entirety of the Bible (both the Old and New Testaments) is fully inspired by God in the original manuscripts, and that it has been kept pure through the centuries of time?

JE: Yes, "The Scripture is the [objective] Word of God."[59] It is "the Word of God, and has nothing in it which is wrong, but is pure and perfect."[60] In the giving of Scripture, there was "an immediate inspiration that the prophets had when they were immediately inspired by the Spirit of God."[61] In the Bible, "it is not men's speaking their own sense of things or interpreting their own minds but the mind of God."[62] The Spirit of God operated in the apostles "infallibly to guide them in points of Christian doctrine."[63]

Just how sure and certain is Scripture?

JE: According to Peter, in 2 Peter 1:19, "the written revelation" that God gives to His church, is "surer than a [divine] voice from heaven."[64]

I know that you reject the mechanical and/or dictation theory of inspiration, wherein the human authors are to be seen as little more than stenographers, and that you believe that God the Holy Spirit acted upon the human authors in an "organic" way, in accordance with their own personalities, characters, temperaments, gifts, and talents.

JE: This is correct. The human authors were the "penmen," who wrote "by the inspiration of the Spirit of God."[65] With regard to the Song of Songs, for example, "I imagine that Solomon when he wrote this song, being a very philosophical, musing man and a pious man, and of a very loving temper, set himself in his own musings to imagine and to point forth to himself a pure, virtuous, pious, and entire love, and represented the musings and feelings of his mind that in a philosophical and religious frame was carried away in a sort of transport, and in that his musings and the train of his imaginations were guided and led on by the Spirit of God. Solomon in his wisdom and great experience had learned the vanity of all other love than of such a sort of one. God's Spirit made use of his loving inclination, joined with his musing philosophical disposition, and so directed and conducted it in this train of imagination as to represent the love that there is between Christ and His spouse."[66]

Moses is another example: "Moses was so intimately conversant with God and so continually under the divine conduct, it cannot be thought that when he wrote the history of the creation and fall of man, and the history of the church from the creation, that he should not be under the divine direction in such an affair. Doubtless he wrote by God's direction, as we are informed that he wrote the law and the history of the Israelitish church."[67]

You would also agree with the Confession *(1:5) that the Bible is a rational revelation, and that there is a "consent of all the parts." Scripture is logically consistent throughout.*

JE: Precisely. There is a "wondrous universal harmony" throughout the Scriptures.[68] For example, "all parts of the Old Testament, though written by so many different penmen and in ages distant one from another, do all harmonize one with all, agree in one, and all center in the same thing, and that a future thing, an event which it was impossible any one of them should know but by divine revelation, even the future coming of Christ."[69] We must remember that "men are reasonable, [and] the Bible does not ask [them] to believe things against reason."[70] "Indeed it is a glorious argument of the divinity of holy Scripture, that they teach such doctrines, which...appear to be exactly agreeable to the most demonstrable, certain, and natural dictates of reason."[71] It is the non-Christian theories which are composed of "a whole heap of inconsistencies."[72]

Furthermore, the "alleged" discrepancies in the Bible are just that: they are "alleged," and nothing more.[73] But there are, of course, "many things in [the Christian] religion and the Scriptures that are made difficult on purpose to try men, and to exercise their faith and scrutiny, and to hinder the proud and self-sufficient."[74]

The Authority and Sufficiency of Scripture

According to your teaching, the full authority and the all-sufficiency of Scripture is due to its unique origin. The Bible is the Word of God, and it has a monopoly on truth. There is no other source of divine, special revelation. The 66 books of the Old and New Testaments are all-sufficient, not only for man to come to a sound and saving knowledge of God, through Jesus Christ, but also to justify all knowledge and to interpret every area of life. Scripture is the sole authority by which all is to be judged. Nothing stands in judgment over the Word of God. Is this an accurate statement?

JE: It is very accurate. "It was God's design, when He

gave the church the Scriptures, so to make and dispose them, and to put so much into them, and in such a manner, that they should be completely sufficient of themselves, that they should hold forth to us things sufficient for us to know, and they should be sufficiently there exhibited, and that in all important matters, whether in doctrine or practice, the Scriptures should sufficiently explain themselves."[75]

But isn't it also true that the inner testimony of the Holy Spirit is necessary to corroborate the authority of the Word of God to fallen man?

JE: "From the Fall of man, to our day, the work of redemption in its effect has mainly been carried on by remarkable communications of the Spirit of God."[76] Many non-believers have an understanding of the Scriptures, but without "the divine and supernatural light, immediately imparted to the soul by the Spirit of God," they never attain a spiritual understanding of the message of Scripture.[77] There is "a spiritual understanding of divine things which all natural and unregenerate men are destitute of."[78] It is "only the Spirit [who] makes them see."[79] It is only the Word of God, as administered by the Spirit of God, which can "subdue the heart" of fallen man.[80]

In this process does the Spirit reveal any new information which causes to reader to believe?

JE: He does not. "This spiritual light is not the suggesting of any new truths or propositions not contained in the Word of God." Rather, the Spirit "gives a due apprehension of those things that are taught in the Word of God."[81]

Scripture and the Individual

We know that in your ministry you stressed the importance of the individual Christian studying the Bible. Just how important is this?

JE: It is essential for growth in the process of sanctification. "The most acceptable way of showing respect to Christ is to give hearty entertainment to the Word."[82] Therefore, "every Christian should make a business of endeavoring to grow in knowledge of divinity [theology].... Divinity comprehends all that is taught in the Scriptures, and so all that we need to know, or is to be known, concerning God and Jesus Christ, concerning our duty to God, and our happiness in God.... There is no other way by which any means of grace whatsoever can be of any benefit, but by knowledge.... Christians ought not to content themselves with such degrees of knowledge in divinity as they have already obtained. It should not satisfy them that they know as much as is absolutely necessary to salvation, but should seek to make progress.... However diligently we apply ourselves, there is room enough to increase our knowledge of divinity, without coming to an end."[83]

Knowing the Bible is one thing; embracing the truths of it is another. Would you not agree with this?

JE: Oh yes. "There are two kinds of knowledge of divine truth, speculative and practical, or in other terms, natural and spiritual. The former remains only in the head. No other faculty but the understanding is concerned with it. It consists of having a natural, or rational knowledge of the things of religion, or such a knowledge as is to be obtained by the natural exercise of our own faculties without any special illumination of the Spirit of God. The latter rests not entirely in the head or in the speculative idea of things, but the heart is concerned in it. It principally consists in the sense of the heart. The mere intellect, without the will or the inclination, is not the seat of it. And it may not only be called seeing, but feeling or tasting. Thus there is a difference between having a right speculative notion of the doctrines contained in the Word of God, and having a due sense of them in the heart. In the former consists the speculative or natural knowledge; in the latter consists the spiritual or practical knowledge. Neither of these is intended in the doctrine exclusive of the other, but it is intended that we should seek the former in order to the latter. The latter, or the spiritual and practical, is of the greatest importance. For a speculative knowledge without a spiritual knowledge is to no purpose but to make our condemnation the greater. Yet a speculative knowledge is also of infinite importance in this respect, that without it we can have no spiritual or practical knowledge."[84]

You are saying, then, that one can have a good degree of speculative knowledge and still be unsaved.

JE: Yes, "there may be a strong belief of divine things in the understanding, and yet no saving faith."[85] "He that has doctrinal knowledge and speculation only, without affections, never is engaged in the business of [Christian] religion."[86] Even the devil "has undoubtedly a great degree of speculative knowledge in divinity, having been, as it were, educated in the best divinity school in the universe, *viz.* the heaven of heavens. The devil is orthodox in his faith; he believes the true scheme of doctrine; he is no Deist, Socinian, Arian, Pelagian, or antinomian; the articles of his faith are all sound, and in them he is thoroughly established."[87]

When you call this kind of knowledge "spiritual knowledge," do you mean that it is a knowledge that comes from God's Spirit?

JE: Exactly; it is "the experiential knowledge of the saving operations of the Holy Spirit."[88]

If Satan and his minions have an orthodox belief concerning God, the Scriptures, the gospel, etc., why do they still turn away from it?

JE: "I answer, that the devils also believe; they know assuredly that the gospel is true; but the devils' and the damned's conviction [arises] not from a sense of God's excellency but only of His greatness."[89]

We know that as a Puritan, you stressed the importance of preaching, for as you have said, "in preaching" there is "the impressing divine things on the heart and affections" of the hearers.[90] *When you speak of the "affections," what are you referring to? Are the affections the same as emotions?*

JE: No, the affections are "no other than the more vigorous and sensible exercises of the inclination and will of the soul.... The will, and the affections of the soul, are not two faculties: the affections are not essentially distinct from the will, nor do they differ from the mere actings of the will and inclination of the soul, but only in the liveliness and sensibleness of exercise."[91]

It is obvious, then, that you do not adhere to the view of "faculty psychology," which maintains that the mind, will, and emotions are separate "faculties" of the one human person. But how then do you explain the human faculties?

JE: "God has indued the soul with two faculties: one is that by which it is capable of perception and speculation, or by which it discerns and views and judges of things; which is called the understanding. The other faculty is that by which the soul does not merely perceive and view things, but is some way inclined with respect to the things it views or considers; either is inclined to them, or is disinclined, and averse from them; or is the faculty by which the soul does not behold things, as an indifferent unaffected spectator; but either as liking or disliking, pleased or displeased, approving or rejecting. This faculty is called by various names: it is sometimes called inclination: and, as it has respect to the actions that are determined and governed by it, is called the will: and the mind, with regard to the exercises of this faculty, is often called the heart."[92]

In what does true religion mainly consist?

JE: "True religion, in great part consists in holy affections.... The holy Scriptures do everywhere place religion very much in the affections; such as fear, hope, hatred, desire, joy, sorrow, gratitude, compassion, zeal." And "affections that are truly spiritual and gracious, do arise from those influences and operations of the heart, which are spiritual, supernatural, and divine." "Those affections which are truly holy, are primarily founded on the loveliness of the moral excellency of divine things."[93]

I believe you are saying that "true religion" is not indifferent to the things of the Christian faith.

JE: Precisely; "true religion consists, in a great measure, in vigorous and lively actings of the inclination of the soul, or the fervent exercises of the heart. That religion which God requires, and will accept, does not consist in weak, dull, and lifeless wishes, raising us but a little above a state of indifference. God, in His Word, greatly insists upon it, that we be in good earnest, fervent in spirit, and our hearts vigorously engaged in religion.... If we be not in good earnest in religion, and our wills and inclinations be not strongly exercised, we are nothing."[94]

While we are on the subject, let me ask you this: Of all of the affections, which is the chief?

JE: "Divine love, or charity, is represented as the sum of all the religion of heaven, and that wherein mainly religion of the church in its more perfect state on earth shall consist...and therefore the higher this holy affection is raised in the church of God, or in a gracious soul, the more excellent and perfect is the state of the church, or a particular soul."[95] "Love...[is] the life, essence, and sum of all true religion." And from this "vigorous, affectionate, and fervent love for God, will necessarily arise other religious affections."[96]

Scripture and the Minister

Tell us something about the work of the minister of the gospel of Jesus Christ.

JE: "Ministers are [God's] messengers, sent forth by Him; and, in their office and administrations among their people, represent His person, stand in His stead, as those that are sent to declare His mind, to do His works, and to speak in

His name."[97] "The work and business of ministers of the gospel is, as it were, that of servants, to wash and cleanse the souls of men; for this is done by the preaching of the Word, which is their main business (Ephesians 5:26)." "One great end and design of God in appointing the gospel ministry is to show His people which is the way of duty."[98] And "it is the duty of ministers of the gospel, in the work of their ministry, to follow the example of their great Lord and Master [Jesus Christ]."[99] "Ministers are not to preach those things which their own wisdom or reason suggests, but the things that are already dictated to them by the superior wisdom and knowledge of God.... [God] holds them [accountable] to go and preach that Word."[100] "It is the excellency of a minister of the gospel to be both a burning and a shining light."[101]

Surely you believe that ministers need to preach both the law and the gospel?

JE: "The gospel is to be preached as well as the law, and the law is to be preached only to make way for the gospel, and in order that it may be preached more effectually. The main work of ministers is to preach the gospel.... So that a minister would miss it very much if he would insist only on the terrors of the law, as to forget his Lord, and neglect to preach the gospel; but yet the law is very much insisted on, and the preaching of the gospel is like to be vain without it."[102]

As an evangelist, surely you did not hesitate to warn your hearers that apart from Christ, they were "sinners in the hands of an angry God."[103]

JE: That is correct. "He that does not believe on the Lord Jesus Christ, the wrath of God abides on him."[104] But "when those that have been earnestly seeking Christ come to find Him they have reason to rejoice with exceeding great joy."[105] There are, however, those "that have seeming come to Christ that do not love Christ above their dearest earthly enjoyments; they are not Christ's disciples."[106] "That which distinguishes the profitable hearers of God's Word from all others is that they [spiritually] understand it and bring forth the fruit of it."[107]

I would further say that "God's Word always comes as conqueror"; "those that are not conquered by conversion shall be conquered by destruction and the execution of its threatenings."[108] Indeed, "there is a great difference between converted and unconverted men."[109] Those who come to savingly believe in Christ, however, must never think that it is of their own doing. Rather, the grace of salvation is the work of God alone: It is "a divine and supernatural light immediately imparted to the soul by the Spirit of God."[110] It is God who "exercises His sovereignty in the eternal salvation of men."[111]

There are some who believe that frequent preaching can be harmful, or at least unprofitable. Yet the Puritans in general believed that it was profitable to preach frequently to "screw" the truth of God's Word into the mind. What is your response to this?

JE: "Such objections against frequent preaching, if they be not from an enmity against religion, are for want of duly considering the way that sermons usually profit an auditory. The *main* benefit that is obtained by preaching is by impression made upon the mind in the time of it, and not by an effect that arises afterwards by a remembrance of what was delivered. And though an after remembrance of what was heard in a sermon is oftentimes very profitable; yet, for the most part, that remembrance is from an impression the words made on the heart in the time of it; and the memory profits as it renews and increases that impression; and a frequent inculcating [of] the more important things of religion in preaching has no tendency to raze out such impressions, but to increase them, and fix them deeper and deeper in the mind."[112]

The Law of God

Reformed theology, as taught in chapter 19 of the Westminster Confession of Faith, *does not separate the law and the gospel, though each is carefully distinguished from the other. Law without gospel is merely a dead letter, but there is no gospel without the law which reveals one's sinful nature and his need for the grace of God in the person and work of Christ. How do you see this?*

JE: I agree with the Westminster divines. The law of God is "exhibited to be as a school master to lead to Christ, not only for the use of that nation [Israel] in the ages of the Old Testament, but for the use of God's church throughout all ages to the end of the world." The law serves "as an instrument that the great Redeemer [Christ] makes use of to convince men of their sin and misery and helplessness and God's awful and tremendous majesty and justice as a lawgiver, and so to make men sensible of the necessity of Christ as a Savior." Further, I also agree with the *Confession* that the moral law also functions as a pattern of life for the regenerate. Here the law is not to be seen "as a covenant of works, but as a rule of life, so it is made use [of] by the Redeemer from that time [the giving of the law at Mount Sinai] to the end of the world as a directory to His people, to show them the way in which they must walk, as they would go to heaven. For a way of sincere and universal obedience to this law is the narrow way that leads to life."[113] "The gospel revelation and dispensation is so far from abating or destroying the perfection of the law...that it vastly increases our obligation to perfect obedience.... No scheme of divinity can be devised or imagined more contrary to the nature, genius, and design of the gospel of Christ, than such a scheme as supposes that the strictness of the law is abated."[114]

Dispensationalists believe that Romans 6:14, where Paul says that "you are not under law but under grace," teaches that the Christian is not under the law of God as a rule of life. How do you respond?

JE: This is a misunderstanding of the verse. Paul is referring to the law as a "covenant of works [which] is not a proper means to bring the fallen creature to the service of God.... A fallen creature held under the covenant of works can't look to

God as a Father and friend." But "those that are redeemed from the bondage of the law, they have great encouragement to serve God [according to the law], in that their poor and imperfect obedience may be accepted.... And He promises that if we will yield ourselves willingly to serve Him as we are able, He will be our friend, and will treat us as a merciful and gracious Father."[115]

As you are aware, the Westminster Confession *also distinguishes the three traditional categories of the law of God: moral, judicial (civil), and ceremonial.*

JE: This also is correct. At Mount Sinai God gave "the typical law in which I suppose [were] included mostly all those precepts that were given to Moses that did not properly belong to the moral law [the Ten Commandments], not only those laws that are commonly called ceremonial in distinction from judicial laws, which are the laws prescribing the ceremonies and circumstances of the Jewish worship and their ecclesiastical state, but also many if not all those divine laws that were political and for regulating the Jewish commonwealth, commonly called judicial laws."[116]

Do you also agree with the teaching of the Confession, *that the moral law, which comprises the Ten Commandments and the "general equity" of the judicial law which God gave to Israel as a nation, is continually binding on men and nations?*

JE: Yes, I do. God's "law is the great rule of righteousness and decorum that the Supreme and Universal Rector has established and published for the regulation of *all* things in the commonwealth of the universality of intelligent beings and moral agents.... It is a rule by which things are not only to be regulated between one subject and another, but between the King and [His] subjects, so that it may be a rule of judgment to the one as well as the rule of duty to the other."[117] "Magistrates," as well as "ministers" of the gospel, and "every living soul, [are] now obliged to arise and acknowledge God in this work" for promoting His kingdom.[118] Surely "it will dispose magistrates to act as the fathers of the commonwealth with that care and concern for the public good which the father of a family has for his household."[119] "When any professing society is as a city set on a hill it is a very great obligation upon them to honor [the Christian] religion in their practice."[120] "God's commands are such as tend greatly to the happiness of men in society. They tend to the good of public societies."[121] This includes the magistrate's responsibility to execute murderers, in accordance with God's law: "God established it as a rule, henceforward to be observed, that murder shall be revenged in a course of public justice."[122]

John Calvin considered the work of the civil magistrate to be of great importance. It appears that you are of the same opinion.

JE: I am. Civil rulers are to be "strong rods" within a community. God tells us that there is a "need of government in societies." God has ordained that good rulers are "vehicles of good to mankind." Scripture even refers to these leaders as "gods." The magistracy is a "great and important business."[123] And men serving in this capacity, should do so as God commands in His law ("as they ought to be"). They are "heads, princes or governors, to whom honor, subjection and obedience should be paid."[124]

What about the ceremonial law?

JE: As far as the ceremonial law is concerned, it was given to Israel as a "typical law." These laws "prescribed the ceremonies and circumstances of the Jewish worship and their ecclesiastical state"; they are no longer binding.[125] These "things of the Old Testament are types of things appertaining to the Messiah, His kingdom, His salvation made manifest from the Old Testament itself."[126] "When Christ died, then there was an end to those types and shadows, because they were then all fulfilled."[127]

So the "believing" Jew saw beyond the ceremonial law to Christ?

JE: Yes. "All the people of Israel, if they exercised consideration, must suppose and understand that these things pertaining to the ceremonial law were appointed and used as representations and symbols of something spiritual, and not for the sake of any innate goodness in them or any value God had for them."[128]

There are scholars who believe that the temple spoken of in Ezekiel 40-48 is a literal temple and means that in an (alleged) future premillennial kingdom the church will actually be offering up "typical" sacrifices, somewhat similar to Old Testament Israel. How do you respond?

JE: "Ezekiel's vision only represents spiritual things, a spiritual temple and spiritual worship that should be in the [New Testament] church." And "this also proves the abolishing of the ceremonial law."[129]

Above you mentioned the word "type." You frequently speak about types. What are types?

JE: "Types are a certain sort of language, as it were, in which God is wont to speak to us. And there is, as it were, a certain idiom in that language which is to be learnt the same that the idiom of any language is, *viz.* by good acquaintance with the language.... God hasn't expressly explained all the types of Scriptures, but has done so much as is sufficient to teach us the language."[130]

Could you give us an example or two?

JE: Sure, "as to marriage, we are expressly taught that that is a designed type of the union between Christ and the church (Ephesians 5:30-32)."[131] Then too, "Jordan is used in Scripture as a type of death, or that change we pass under in going out of this world into an eternal state."[132]

What about numbers as symbols, such as the number "seven?" Is this not the number of perfection?

JE: Yes. "The reason why the number 'seven' is everywhere put for perfection, is because in seven days all things were perfected and completed, both as to work and rest. So that the seventh number as well as the seventh day, is sanctified, that is, has a note of perfection put on it everywhere in Scripture."[133]

---

[1] Edwards, *Works*, I:xxi.
[2] Edwards, *Works*, II:481-482.
[3] Edwards, *Works* (Yale), 9.
[4] Edwards, *Works* (Yale), 9:116.
[5] Edwards, *Miscellany* 1353.
[6] Edwards, *Sermon* on Matthew 5:44.
[7] Edwards, *Sermon* on Hebrews 9:15-16.
[8] Edwards, *Sermon* on Romans 9:18.
[9] Edwards, *Works*, I:533.
[10] Edwards, *Works* (Yale), 4:533.
[11] Edwards, *Miscellany* 786.
[12] Edwards, *Miscellany* 1091.
[13] Edwards, *Miscellany* 695.
[14] Edwards, *Works*, II:599.
[15] Edwards, *Works* (Yale), 3:348.
[16] Edwards, *Sermon* on Genesis 3:11.
[17] Edwards, *Miscellany* 1078.
[18] Edwards, *Miscellany* 884.
[19] Edwards, *Miscellany* 285.
[20] Edwards, *Sermon* on Romans 4:16.
[21] Edwards, *Miscellany* 717.
[22] Edwards, *Works*, II:599.
[23] Edwards, *Miscellany* 825.
[24] Edwards, *Works* (Yale), 9:132-133.
[25] Edwards, *Works*, I:537.
[26] Edwards, *Works* (Yale), 9:132ff., 172.
[27] Edwards, *Works* (Yale), 9:138.
[28] Edwards, *Works* (Yale), 15:302.
[29] Edwards, *Works* (Yale), 15:533.
[30] Edwards, *Works* (Yale), 12:279.
[31] Edwards, *Sermon* on Isaiah 55:3.
[32] Edwards, *Miscellany* 1353.
[33] Edwards, *Works* (Yale), 9:290.

[34] Edwards, *Sermon* on John 14:27.
[35] Edwards, *Works* (Yale), 9:442-443.
[36] Edwards, *Miscellany* 299.
[37] Edwards, *Miscellany* 617.
[38] Edwards, *Miscellany* 993.
[39] Edwards, *Works* (Yale), 9:117-119.
[40] Edwards, *Sermon* on Hebrews 13:8.
[41] Edwards, *Works* (Yale), 21:136.
[42] Edwards, *Sermon* on Hebrews 9:15-16.
[43] Edwards, *Miscellany* 1064.
[44] Edwards, *Works* (Yale), 15:367.
[45] Edwards, *Sermon* on Joshua 7:12.
[46] Edwards, *Sermon* on Proverbs 14:34.
[47] Edwards, *Sermon* on Romans 12:18.
[48] Edwards, *Sermon* on 2 Chronicles 25:9.
[49] Edwards, *Miscellany* 358.
[50] Edwards, *Works* (Yale), 4:434.
[51] Edwards, *Miscellany* 358.
[52] Cited in Grosart, *Selections From the Unpublished Writings of Jonathan Edwards,* 193.
[53] Edwards, *Works* (Yale), 9:273.
[54] Edwards, *Charity and Its Fruits,* 310.
[55] Edwards, *Charity and Its Fruits,* 304-322.
[56] Edwards, *Sermon* on 1 Corinthians 13:8-13.
[57] Edwards, *Works* (Yale), 9:365-370.
[58] Edwards, *Works* (Yale), 2:111.
[59] Edwards, *Sermon* on 2 Timothy 3:16.
[60] Edwards, *Works* (Yale), 2:143.
[61] Edwards, *Miscellany* 20.
[62] Cited in Gerstner, *The Rational Biblical Theology of Jonathan Edwards,* I:142.
[63] Edwards, *Works,* II:265.
[64] Edwards, *Works* (Yale), 15:217.
[65] Edwards, *Works* (Yale), 15:518-520.
[66] Edwards, *Miscellany* 303.
[67] Edwards, *Miscellany* 352.
[68] Edwards, *Miscellany* 333.
[69] Edwards, *Works* (Yale), 9:283.
[70] Edwards, *Sermon* on Isaiah 3:10.
[71] Edwards, *Works* (Yale), I:439.
[72] Edwards, *Works,* I:30.
[73] Edwards, *Works,* II:676ff.
[74] Edwards, *Miscellany* 139.
[75] Edwards, *Miscellany* 535.
[76] Edwards, *Works,* I:539.

[77] Edwards, *Sermon* on Matthew 16:17.
[78] Edwards, *Sermon* on 1 Corinthians 2:14.
[79] Edwards, *Sermon* on 2 Corinthians 3:18.
[80] Edwards, *Sermon* on Jeremiah 23:29.
[81] Edwards, *Sermon* on Matthew 16:17.
[82] Edwards, *Sermon* on Luke 10:38-42.
[83] Edwards, *Sermon* on Hebrews 5:12.
[84] Edwards, *Sermon* on Hebrews 5:12.
[85] Edwards, *Works* (Yale), 21:442.
[86] Edwards, *Works* (Yale), 2:101.
[87] Edwards, *Works*, II:43.
[88] Edwards, *Sermon* on 1 Corinthians 2:14.
[89] Edwards, *Miscellany* 369.
[90] Edwards, *Works* (Yale), 2:115.
[91] Edwards, *Works* (Yale), 2:96-97.
[92] Edwards, *Works* (Yale), 2:96.
[93] Edwards, *Works* (Yale), 2:95ff.; 197, 253ff.
[94] Edwards, *Religious Affections*, 27-28.
[95] Edwards, *Works* (Yale), 2:299.
[96] Edwards, *Works* (Yale), 2:146, 108.
[97] Edwards, *Sermon* on 2 Corinthians 1:14.
[98] Edwards, *Sermon* on Isaiah 30:20-21.
[99] Edwards, *Sermon* on John 13:15-16.
[100] Edwards, *Sermon* on 1 Corinthians 2:11-13.
[101] Edwards, Sermon on John 5:35.
[102] Edwards, *Works*, II:266.
[103] Edwards, *Sermon* on Deuteronomy 32:25.
[104] Edwards, *Sermon* on John 3:36.
[105] Edwards, *Sermon* on Matthew 2:10.
[106] Edwards, *Sermon* on Luke 14:26.
[107] Edwards, *Sermon* on Matthew 13:23.
[108] Edwards, *Works* (Yale), 5:105.
[109] Edwards, *Sermon* on Matthew 15:26.
[110] Edwards, *Sermon* on Matthew 16:17.
[111] Edwards, *Sermon* on Romans 9:18.
[112] Edwards, *Works* (Yale), 4:397.
[113] Edwards, *Works* (Yale), 9:180-181.
[114] Edwards, *Works* (Yale), 21:340-341.
[115] Edwards, *Works* (Yale), 15:198.
[116] Edwards, *Works* (Yale), 9:181.
[117] Cited in *Our Great and Glorious God*, 178.
[118] Edwards, *Works*, I:389.
[119] Edwards, *Charity and Its Fruits*, 170.
[120] Edwards, *Sermon* on Matthew 5:14.

[121] Edwards, *Sermon* on Deuteronomy 10:13.
[122] Edwards, *Works* (Yale), 15:328-329.
[123] Edwards, *Sermon* on Ezekiel 19:12.
[124] Edwards, *Miscellany* 336.
[125] Edwards, *Works* (Yale), 9:169.
[126] Edwards, *Miscellany* 1439.
[127] Edwards, *Works* (Yale), 15:325.
[128] Edwards, *Works* (Yale), 11:307.
[129] Edwards, *Miscellany* 1104.
[130] Edwards, *Works* (Yale), 11:150-151.
[131] Edwards, *Works* (Yale), 11:53.
[132] Edwards, *Works* (Yale), 15:358.
[133] Edwards, *Works* (Yale), 5:97.

CHAPTER 5
Edwards on God

Certainly we are justified in saying that just as the doctrine of God is central to the teaching of Scripture, so also this doctrine is central to the Christian worldview.

JE: Yes, this is correct. "The Being of God is reckoned the first, greatest and most fundamental of all things that are the objects of knowledge or belief."[1] "God is the sum of all being, and there is no being without His being. All things are in Him, and He in all."[2] "God is infinitely exalted in gloriousness and excellency above all created things."[3] "God is...the head of the universal system of existence; the foundation and fountain of all being and all beauty; from whom all is perfectly derived, and on whom all is most absolutely and perfectly dependent."[4] He is "the supreme Harmony of all."[5]

When you speak of God being "the sum of all being," and say that "all things are in Him, and He in all," it is possible that some would accuse you of being a Pantheist.[6] *How would you respond?*

JE: I am not a Pantheist. We must always distinguish between "God and His creatures," between "the Creator and all His creatures."[7] "God is God, and distinguished from all other beings, and exalted above them."[8]

Let's talk for a bit, Mr. Edwards, about the doctrine of God. Theologians, such as those who wrote the Westminster Standards, normally subdivide the study of God into the being of God and the works of God.[9] *The former has to do with who God is; the latter studies what He does.*

The Being of God

The Westminster Shorter Catechism *(Q. 4-6) defines God as follows:*

> God is a Spirit, infinite, eternal, and unchangeable, in His being, wisdom, power, holiness, justice, goodness, and truth.... There is but one [God] only, the living and true God.... There are three persons in the Godhead: the Father, the Son, and the Holy Ghost; and these three are one God, the same in substance [i.e., essence], equal in power and glory.

I assume that you are in basic agreement with this definition?

JE: I am. I have stated that "God is infinitely, eternally, unchangeably, and independently glorious and perfect." In God there is "infinite power, wisdom, righteousness, goodness...[and] truth." He is the all-sufficient God, who "stands in no need of, cannot be profited by, or receive anything from the creature."[10] God "is the infinite, universal and all comprehending existence."[11] "God is a being possessed of the most absolutely perfect happiness."[12]

Sometimes it is said that God is incomprehensible. What does this mean?

JE: It means that "we may have a true knowledge of God, though not a comprehensive [exhaustive] knowledge of Him."[13]

Is it proper to say that God is defined by means of His attributes; that He is the totality of His attributes; or that He is identical with His attributes?

JE: This is a very proper way of saying it, because God is "universal Being...the eternal and infinite Being."[14] "The attributes of God are God."[15]

The Attributes of God

For ease of study, theologians sometimes distinguish between the attributes of God. Do you think that this is helpful?

JE: I do. For example, theologians "make a distinction between the natural and moral perfections of God. By the moral perfections of God they mean those attributes which God exercises as a moral agent: His righteousness, truth, faithfulness, and goodness; or in a word, His holiness. By God's natural attributes or perfections they mean those attributes, according to our way of conceiving God, that consist of His greatness, His power, His knowledge, His eternal being, His omnipresence, and His awful and terrible majesty."[16] These two comprise "the glorious attributes of God."[17] Of the two, however, the moral attributes are more excellent. The reason being that "strength and knowledge do not render any being lovely, without holiness; but more hateful: though they render them more lovely when joined with holiness."[18]

Please tell us about some of the attributes of God, beginning with His natural attributes.

JE: I would be glad to do so, but as we do so, let us first understand that "God is the prime and original being, the first and last, and the pattern of all, and has the sum of all perfection."[19]

Natural Attributes

Infinity

JE: The God of the Bible is "the supreme and infinite being."[20] He is "necessary" Being.[21] He is that "Being whose loveliness, honorableness, and authority are infinite."[22] When we speak of God's infinity with regard to space, we refer to His omnipresence. "God is everywhere present with His all seeing eye.... He is present by His knowledge and essence."[23] God is "the Supreme Being" who "fills heaven and earth."[24] But God is also distinct from His creation. He is infinite in His transcendence; He is not restricted by space and time. "God is infinitely exalted in gloriousness and excellency above all created beings."[25] And there is an "infinite happiness" that exists between the persons of the Trinity.[26]

We know that God is omnipresent, but where is His principle abode?

JE: "Heaven is a part of the universe that, in the first creation and disposition of things that was made in the beginning, was appropriated to God to be that part of the universe that should be His residence, while all other parts were destined to other uses." In fact, "heaven is so much the proper place of God's abode that by a metonymy heaven is put for God Himself [Psalm 73:9; Luke 15:21]."[27]

Eternality

JE: When we speak of God's infinity with regard to time, we refer to His eternality. God has always been and always will be. He "is eternal by the necessity of His own nature."[28] With God there is "eternal duration, it being without succession, present, before, and after."[29] "He is an independent Being, for He, being the first Being and an eternal Being, must be an independent Being."[30]

Aseity

JE: As expressed in His name, "I Am That I Am," God is completely independent and self-sufficient.[31] "God is the sum of all being."[32]

The name of God is very important in biblical Christianity, is it not?

JE: Oh yes, it is. God "Himself is His name, and His name is Himself."[33]

Simplicity

JE: There is an absolute unity in God, a "perfect and absolute simplicity."[34] So much is this the case, that we may say that "God and real existence are the same." Therefore, "we learn how properly it may be said that God is and that there is none else, and how proper are these names of the

Deity: '*Jehovah*,' and 'I Am That I Am.'"[35] The simplicity and/or unity of God, who is pure Spirit, also assures us that each and every one of God's attributes is identical with His being, as "He is the sum of all perfection."[36]

Immutability

JE: The triune God is "immutable." "God never changes His mind.... God is in Himself but one simple and pure act."[37] Further, God's attribute of immutability also assures us that His promises can never fail: "God never fails in any instance of His faithfulness to the covenant engagements He has entered into in behalf of mankind."[38] The unchangeable nature of God does not mean, however, that He is a static being; rather, He is dynamic and active, working in His created order.[39]

You say that God does not change His mind, but the Scripture sometimes speaks of God's repenting, e.g., in Genesis 6:6 ("God repented that He had made man").

JE: "But the meaning is not that God had changed His mind, but only that He acted differently or produced a different effect as men are wont to do when they repent. He did not properly repent that He had made man on the earth. He did not alter His mind and think that it would have been best never to have made man. But He is now of the mind that it is best that man should be allowed to be on the earth no longer —and He acts as men do when they repent."[40]

Does God emote?

JE: No, an immutable being cannot emote. "There is no such thing truly as any pain, or grief, or trouble in God."[41]

You have said that the immutability of God is the attribute that non-believers hate more than any other. Why is this?

JE: Because non-believers know that "this attribute assures them that God will never change in His hatred of them and their sins; neither will He ever change His mind about their damnation."[42]

Truth

JE: "God is truth itself."[43] This being so, if we are to know the truth, we must know what is in the mind of God: "the consistency and agreement of our ideas [must agree] with the ideas of God."[44]

Sovereignty

JE: God is absolutely sovereign over all aspects of reality, both the material and the spiritual. "Absolute sovereignty is what I love to ascribe to God."[45] "God is…the Supreme Regulator and Rector of the universe, the orderer of things relating to the whole compass of existence, including Himself."[46] The God of Scripture is all-powerful; He "is infinitely strong."[47] The destiny of all men rests in the hands of almighty God: "The sovereignty of God is His absolute, independent right of disposing of all creatures according to His own pleasure."[48] "God does whatever He pleases…. [And] He is able to do everything that doesn't apply [imply] a contradiction to itself or to His own holy nature."[49]

I believe that (technically) there is a difference between God's sovereignty and His omnipotence.

JE: Yes, there is. In Daniel 4, "Nebuchadnezzar acknowledges that God's power is twofold: One is a power of ability, whereby He is able to do what He pleases; the other is His power of right, whereby He has a right to do what He pleases. One [the former] is His strength and the other [the latter] is His sovereignty."[50]

Omniscience

JE: The triune God of the Bible is all wise; He eternally knows all things completely and exhaustively. His knowledge of all things past, present, and future, is all comprehensive. Such knowledge renders the future certain and necessary, thereby ruling out all contingency.[51] God's is a "perfect wisdom," a "perfect knowledge," which is "far above" the wisdom of any creature.[52] And whereas the knowledge possessed by the creature is "discursive," "temporal," and "incomplete," God's knowledge is "intuitive," "original," "timeless," and "complete."[53]

There is an age-old question regarding the omniscience of God: Does God know all things because He decrees all things, or does He decree all things because He knows all things?

JE: "God must know all things because He decrees all things."[54]

In Romans 8:29, Paul speaks about the foreknowledge of God. How does the apostle use this word?

JE: In this verse, "God's eternal foreknowledge is the same with God's eternal election of them [the elect] or choosing them from eternity to be His."[55] And it is "in the work of redemption" that we see the "wisdom of God" most clearly displayed.[56]

How would you respond to the view of the "open theists" who believe that God does not have an exhaustive foreknowledge of all things, most specifically the free actions of men?

JE: "God has an absolute and certain foreknowledge of the free actions of moral agents.... One would think [that] it should be wholly needless to enter on such an argument with any that profess themselves Christians."[57]

Moral Attributes

JE: The moral attributes of God are more excellent, i.e., "more lovely" than the natural attributes, because without the moral excellency of God, i.e., the holiness of God, the natural attributes would not be "lovely" at all. Omnipotence and omniscience by themselves do not make God a "lovely," "holy" being. But when the natural attributes are understood as "holy" attributes, then they are "lovely." Therefore, "a true love to God for the beauty of His moral attributes, necessarily causes delight for all His attributes; for His moral attributes cannot be without His natural attributes. Infinite holiness supposes infinite wisdom and infinite greatness; and all the attributes of God as it were imply one another."[58]

Holiness

JE: The God of Scripture is "an infinitely holy God." This holiness is the "excellency and beauty of God's nature whereby His heart is disposed and delights in everything that is morally good and excellent."[59] "God is an infinitely holy being."[60] This is why the saints "love God in the first place because the beauty of His holiness or His moral perfection is supremely lovable in itself."[61] "His holiness is such as will not and cannot endure the least impurity or filthiness."[62] "When God is loved aright He is loved for His excellency, the beauty of His nature, especially the holiness of His nature."[63] "A sight of God's loveliness must begin...with a delight in His holiness...for no other attribute is truly lovely without this," because "the beauty of the divine nature does primarily consist in God's holiness."[64] "The holiness of God has always appeared to me the most lovely of all His attributes."[65]

Somewhat parenthetically, you frequently speak of the "beauty" of God.

JE: Yes, I do, because beauty is "wherein the truest idea of divinity does consist." "God is God, and distinguished from all other beings, and exalted above them, chiefly by His divine beauty, which is infinitely diverse from all other beauty." And "holiness is in a peculiar manner the beauty of the divine nature."[66]

Love

JE: The love of God is sometimes considered as "the same thing" as His holiness.[67] And God's love for His creatures should be seen as two-fold. First, there is a love of benevolence, which is a creational love that extends to all of God's creatures. Even the ungodly have a share in this love of God: "God provides some proper good for the satisfaction of the appetites and desires of every living thing."[68] "God is kind to the unthankful and evil."[69] And second, there is God's love of complacency, which extends only to the elect. It is an everlasting love, which involves the redeeming cross work of Jesus Christ; and it is a mercy that could only be bestowed upon the elect by Him.[70] "Love is commonly distinguished into a love of complacence and a love of benevolence. Of these two a love of complacence is first, and is the foundation of the other, if by a love of complacence is meant the relishing a sweetness in the qualifications of the beloved, and being pleased and delighted in his excellency. This, in the order of nature, is before benevolence, because it is the foundation and reason for it."[71]

Furthermore, since God loves infinitely, "there must have been an object from all eternity, which God infinitely loves." And "the object which God infinitely loves, must be infinitely perfectly consenting…to Him; but that which infinitely and perfectly agrees is the very same essence." This, of course, is the self-love which eternally exists among the Trinity.[72] And the Holy Spirit is intimately involved in "the act of God between the Father and the Son infinitely loving and delighting in each other."[73]

Justice

JE: The God of the Bible always acts with perfect justice and righteousness: "Nothing is more precisely according to the truth of things, than divine justice; it weighs things in an even balance; it views and estimates things no otherwise than they are truly in their own nature."[74] The triune God "is a just and righteous God." "God's faithfulness is part of His holiness, and this is what is meant by righteousness."[75]

I assume that this means that God's attribute of justice includes His wrath against all evil. He hates evil and must punish it. Isn't this so?

JE: Yes, it is. He "has sworn that He will be revenged on wicked men." The justice of God in the day of judgment "will appear strict, exact, awful, and terrible, and therefore [it will be] glorious."[76] Further, "it is requisite that God should punish sin with infinite punishment; because all sin, as it is against God, is infinitely heinous, and has infinite demerit."[77]

Does this mean that just one sin is worthy of such punishment?

JE: Yes, if a person "trespasses in one point, is guilty of any of the least sin, he, according to the law of God…is exposed to be wholly cast out of favor with God, and subjected to His curse, to be utterly and eternally destroyed."[78]

Does God hate sinners?

JE: Yes, He does. We must not err here and say that God hates the sin, but loves the sinner. God "abhors persons for their sins."[79] "While men are under the dominion of sin and held under the guilt of it, God loathes them. They are more abominable in the sight of God than toads, serpents, or the vilest vermin. Every wicked man is loathed and abhorred by God."[80]

Is it also true that these sinners hate God?

JE: It is. "Wicked men have an abhorrence of God." "There is a mutual loathing and abhorrence between God and wicked men."[81]

Glory

In your writing you often associate the "glory" of God with His attributes, both natural and moral.[82] *How do you respond to this?*

JE: Sometimes the word "glory, as applied to God…signifies the communication of His fullness." Other times "glory, as applied to God in Scripture implies the view or knowledge of God's excellency." "It is [also] manifest that God's name and His glory, at least very often, signify the same thing in Scripture."[83]

How does one see the glory of God?

JE: "The discovery of God's spiritual glory is not by immediate intuition, but the Word of God is the medium by which it is discovered. It is by God's proclaiming His name; so God reveals Himself to the saints in this world by proclaiming His name in the joyful sound of the gospel."[84]

You do believe, do you not, that all things that occur in this universe take place for the purpose of glorifying God?

JE: Definitely so. The glory of God "is fitly compared to an effulgence or emanation of light from a luminary, by which the glory of God is abundantly represented in Scripture. Light is the external expression, exhibition and manifestation of the excellency of the luminary, of the sun for instance; it is the abundant, extensive emanation and communication of the fullness of the sun to innumerable beings that partake of it.... The beams of glory come from God, and are something of God, and are refunded back again to their original. So that the whole is of God, and in God, and to God; and God is the beginning, middle and end of this affair."[85]

How does the glory of God affect His creatures?

JE: "God's glory, as it is spoken of in Scripture as the end of all of God's works, is in the emanation of that fullness of God that is from eternity in God, *ad extra*, and towards those creatures that are capable of being sensible and active objects of such an emanation. It consists in communicating Himself to those two faculties of the understanding and will, by which faculties it is that creatures are sensible and active objects or subjects of divine emanations and communications.... So the glory of God is the shining forth or effulgence of His perfections, or the communication of His perfections, as effulgence is the communication of light."[86]

Should all things in the created world be seen as a reflection of God's glory?

JE: Yes, this is so. "For indeed the whole outward creation, which is but the shadows of beings, is so made as to represent spiritual things. It might be demonstrated by the wonderful agreement in thousands of things, much of the same kind as in between the types of the Old Testament and their antitypes, and by spiritual things being so often and continually compared with them in the Word of God. And it's agreeable to God's wisdom that it should be so, that the inferior and shadowy parts of His work should be made to represent those things that are more real and excellent, spiritual and divine, to represent the things that immediately concern Himself and the highest parts of His work. Spiritual things are the crown and glory, the head and soul, the very end and Alpha and Omega of all other works: what therefore can be more agreeable to wisdom, than that they should be so made as to shadow them forth?"[87]

The Trinity

Let's discuss the Trinity.

JE: That's fine. "God has appeared glorious to me, on account of the Trinity. It has made me have exalting thoughts of God that He subsists in three persons: Father, Son, and Holy Ghost."[88] The Trinity is "the supreme harmony of all."[89]

As we have seen, the Westminster Shorter Catechism *(Q. 5-6), teaches that "there is but one only, the living and true God," and that "there are three persons in the Godhead; the Father, the Son, and the Holy Ghost; and these three are one God, the same in substance, equal in power and glory." And you agree with this teaching.*

JE: Correct; "all the persons of the Trinity are in exact equality as we are taught in the *Catechism* those three are the same substance equal in power and glory."[90] The one true and living God of Scripture "subsists in three persons: Father, Son, and Holy Ghost." And all three members of the Godhead are equally and eternally divine, i.e., "the whole divine essence is supposed truly and properly to subsist in each of these three."[91] Ontologically, "the persons of the Trinity are equal among themselves."[92] "They are every way equal in the society or family of the three," and "they are all God."[93]

We must never think, then, that there are three gods (tri-theism).

JE: No, "we do not suppose that the Father, the Son, and the Holy Ghost are three distinct beings that have three distinct understandings."[94] We must not think of the "Father, Son, and Holy Ghost as three distinct gods, friends to one another."[95]

Theologians often use the term perichoresis *when speaking about the Trinity, to speak about the mutual participation and co-inherence among the persons of the Godhead. Do you hold to this view?*

JE: I do. "In order to clear up this matter, let it be considered, that the whole divine essence is supposed truly and properly to subsist in each of these three—*viz.* God, and His understanding, and love—and that there is such a wonderful union between them that they are after an ineffable and inconceivable manner one in another; so that one has another, and they have communion in one another, and are as it were predicable one of another. As Christ said of Himself and the Father, 'I am in the Father, and the Father in me [John 14:10], so may it be said concerning all the persons of the Trinity: the Father is in the Son, and the Son is in the Father; the Holy Ghost is in the Father, and the Father in the Holy Ghost; the Holy Ghost is in the Son, and the Son in the Holy Ghost."[96]

Further, the Westminster Confession *teaches that each of the three persons in the Godhead has distinguishing properties. The differences between the persons are not differences in essence; they are merely distinctions within the Trinity.*

JE: This is so; "the personal glory of each of the persons in the Trinity is equal, though each one, as they have a distinct personality, have a distinct glory, and so one has a peculiar glory that another has not."[97]

In typical orthodox fashion, the Confession *(2:3) says that "the Father is of none, neither begotten, nor proceeding; the Son is eternally begotten of the Father; the Holy Ghost eternally proceeding from the Father and the Son." Simply stated, that which distinguishes the three members is the eternal paternity of the Father, the eternal Sonship of the Son, and the eternal procession of the Spirit. Is this correct?*

JE: Yes, I agree with this statement; it correctly speaks of "the [eternal] generation of the Son" and "the [eternal] proceeding of the Holy Ghost."[98] But I would enlarge on this by stating that the eternal begotteness of the Son consists in the Father's having a perfect idea of Himself, which is the Son: "The image of God which God infinitely loves and has His chief delight in, is the perfect idea of God,...[which is] the perfect idea of Himself." And the "Scriptures tell us that the Son of God is that image." And I would further state that the Holy Spirit, as "eternal love," is that member of the Trinity who eternally proceeds from the Father and the Son in an act of divine and "infinite love and delight" that exists between them.[99] "God is glorified within Himself these two ways: 1) By appearing, or being manifested to Himself in His own perfect idea; or in the Son, who is the brightness of His glory; 2) By enjoying and delighting in Himself, by flowing forth in infinite love and delight towards Himself; or in His Holy Spirit."[100] Or, said another way: "The Son is the Deity generated by God's understanding, or having an idea of Himself; the Holy Ghost is the divine essence flowing out, or breathed forth, in infinite love and delight. Or, which is the same, the Son is God's idea of Himself, and the Spirit is God's love to and delight in Himself."[101]

Simply stated, are you saying that the Father has eternally been the Father, the Son has eternally been the Son, and the Holy Spirit has eternally been the Holy Spirit?

JE: Yes, I am. "And this I suppose to be the blessed Trinity that we read of in the Holy Scriptures. The Father is the

Deity subsisting in the prime, unoriginated and most absolute manner, or the Deity in its direct existence. The Son is the Deity generated by God's understanding, or having an idea of Himself and subsisting in that idea. The Holy Ghost is the Deity subsisting in act, or the divine essence flowing out and breathed forth in God's infinite love to and delight in Himself. And I believe the whole divine essence does truly and distinctly subsist both in the divine idea and divine love, and that each of them" is a properly distinct person.[102]

You do believe, do you not, that there is an order of economy, or administration, within the Godhead, which is generally referred to as the economic Trinity?

JE: Assuredly, I do. "There is a subordination of the persons of the Trinity, in their actings with respect to the creature; that one acts from another, and under another, and with a dependence on another, in their actings, and particularly in what they act in the affair of man's redemption. So that the Father in that affair acts as the Head of the Trinity, and the Son under Him, and the Holy Spirit under them both."[103] We also see this in the work of creation, making man in His own image: "The Father employed the Son and the Holy Ghost in this work. The Son endued men with understanding and reason. The Holy Ghost endued him with a holy will and inclination with original righteousness."[104]

And in this relationship there is a form of subordinationism, but the subordination is not in the essence of the members of the Trinity, but in the function or role that each member has to perform in redemptive history?

JE: Yes, "hence we may better understand the economy of the persons of the Trinity as it appears in the part that each one has in the affair of redemption."[105] This "order [or] economy of the persons of the Trinity [is] with respect to their actions *ad extra*."[106] And "all the persons of the Trinity do concur in all acts *ad extra.*"[107] "The Father is before the Son [but] not of subordination."[108]

The Works of God

Reformed theology in general maintains that the works of God are determined by His decrees, and that these works can be summarized under the headings of creation and providence. Do you agree?

JE: I do.

The Decrees of God

According to the Westminster Shorter Catechism *(Q. 7), "the decrees of God are, His eternal purpose, according to the counsel of His will, whereby, for His own glory, He has foreordained whatsoever comes to pass." Is this also your view?*

JE: Yes. "All that is intended when we say that God decrees all that comes to pass is that all events are subject to the disposals of divine providence, or that God orders all things in His providence, that He intended from eternity to order all things in providence, and intended to order them as He does."[109] "God decrees all things from all eternity."[110] And "all of the decrees of God are harmonious."[111]

And what is the end for which God decrees the things He does?

JE: "All that is ever spoken of in Scripture as an ultimate end of God's works, is included in the one phrase, the glory of God."[112]

How far-reaching are the decrees of God?

JE: So sovereign is God in His decretive will, that all of the days of every man, woman, and child are both numbered and "precisely decreed to the hour, minute, second." And man "can do nothing to change it." "God unalterably determines the limit of men's life."[113]

Does the sovereignty of God in His decretive purposes extend even to the Fall of man, and all other sins as well?

JE: It does. "God has decreed every action of men, yea,

[even] every action that is sinful and every circumstance of those actions." Sin "is foreordained in God's decrees, and ordered in providence.... God decrees all things, and even all sins."[114] "God decreed from all eternity to permit all evil that ever He does permit...nothing can come to pass but what it is the will and pleasure of God should come to pass."[115]

This means that nothing in the universe occurs by chance. There are no contingent events; there is no such thing as luck or fate. All things that have ever taken place, or that will ever take place, occur as a result of God's sovereign decretive will; which will is the first cause and governing factor of all things.

JE: That is absolutely true, as I point out in my *The Freedom of the Will.*

Does this not make God the author of sin?

JE: No, it does not. God "orders" sin, but does not "author" it.[116]

You are aware of the Arminian claim that if God's decree renders the certainty of sin being committed, then this would take away all liberty and make the warnings and exhortations of Scripture nothing more than an illusion. How do you respond to this?

JE: "To this I would bring the instance of Peter. Christ told him that he would surely deny Him thrice that night before the cock should crow twice. And yet, after that, Christ exhorted all His disciples to watch and pray so that they might not fall into temptation."[117]

You are also aware that some consider the view you are espousing to make God arbitrary. How do you respond?

JE: The acts of God are arbitrary. But by "arbitrary" what I mean is "that which depends on nothing but the divine will; which divine will depends on nothing but the divine wisdom."[118] "It is the glory of God that He is an arbitrary being...[and] acts as being limited and directed in nothing but His own wisdom."[119]

When it comes to the decrees of God, it seems that your main emphasis is on the eternal destiny of mankind.

JE: That is true. God's attribute of sovereignty necessitates "His absolute, independent right of disposing of all creatures according to His own pleasure."[120] "God is sometimes in Scripture spoken of as taking pleasure in punishing men's sins." And "God is often spoken of as exercising goodness and showing mercy."[121] God has "mercy on whom He will have mercy, and whom He will, He hardens."[122]

Are divine election and reprobation determined by God's foreknowledge of the thoughts or choices of man?

JE: No. "God's loving some and not others [is] antecedent to any manner of difference in them."[123]

What you are espousing here is the Reformed doctrine of double predestination.

JE: Correct. God "has absolutely determined who shall be saved and who shall be damned."[124] Divine election necessitates divine reprobation.[125]

In accord with Deuteronomy 29:29, classical Reformed orthodoxy distinguishes between God's decretive or secret will and His preceptive or revealed will. The former determines all things that will ever occur. The latter, on the other hand, is revealed in God's Word, which men are enjoined to obey. Whereas the decretive will is hidden in the mind of God, and is absolute, and determined by God alone, the preceptive will is that will of God for man, which man is to live by. Man is accountable for the preceptive will, not the decretive will. But this has caused a problem for many persons. How do you view this?

JE: "When a distinction is made between God's revealed will and His secret will, or His will of command and decree, will is certainly in that distinction taken in two senses. His will of decree, is not His will in the same sense as His will of command is. Therefore, it is no difficulty at all to suppose that the one may be otherwise than the other. His will in both senses is His inclination. But when we say He wills virtue, or loves virtue, or the happiness of His creature; thereby is intended, that virtue, or the creature's happiness, absolutely and simply considered, is agreeable to the inclination of His nature. His will of decree is, His inclination to a thing, not as that thing absolutely and simply, but with respect to the universality of things that have been, are, or shall be. So God, though He hates a thing as it is simply, may incline to it with reference to the universality of things. Though He hates sin in itself, yet He may will to permit it, for the greater promotion of holiness in this universality, including all things, and at all times."[126]

Is there any such thing as the laws of nature?

JE: Yes; but what "we call the laws of nature" are only "the stated methods of God's acting with respect to bodies."[127]

Of all of God's works, which is the greatest?

JE: "The work of redemption is so much the greatest of all the works of God, that all other works are to be looked upon either as part of it, or appendages to it...for the work of redemption is the great subject of the whole Bible."[128] Or to say it another way, "the creation of all things was with an aim and subordination to that great work of Christ as Mediator, *viz.* the work of redemption."[129] "The world was created that Christ might obtain a spouse."[130]

God's foreordination of the Fall, then, was a good thing.

JE: Yes, the elect are more greatly benefited. Elect man has "been brought to a state vastly better than its former being before the Fall.... So that hereby God acquires an infinitely great and strong right to the redeemed; for the right is equal to the expense that obtained it, since that expense was necessary, and the benefit of the redeemed equal to the expense; which is not only to the glory of God, but will be a matter of rejoicing to the redeemed, to think that God has so great a right to them, and will make [them], with so much the more earnestness of consent and desire, yield themselves to God, and devote themselves to serve and glorify Him."[131]

Creation

According to the Westminster Shorter Catechism *(Q. 9), "the work of creation is, God's making all things of nothing, by the word of His power, in the space of six days, and all very good." Are you in agreement with this teaching?*

JE: I am.

Do you hold to a six solar day creation?

JE: Yes, I do. There were "six days…of creation…and the seventh…was the Sabbath."[132]

Does this teaching of the Catechism *mean that the world came out of nothing?*

JE: No, the creation came from the eternal propositions in the mind of God.[133] "Though these exercises of God [in creation]…are in time…. They were always equally present in the divine mind."[134]

Clearly we understand that the creation itself cannot add anything to the ever blessed God.

JE: Correct; "God stands in no need of creatures and is not profited by them; neither can His happiness be said to be added to by the creature."[135]

Why then did God create the world?

JE: Ultimately, of course, "the end of the creation is that the creation might glorify [God]."[136] "God made all things; and the end for which all things are made, and for which they are disposed, and for which they work continually, is that God's glory may shine forth and be received."[137] "The great and universal end of God's creating the world was to communicate Himself. God is a communicating Being. [But] this communication is really only to intelligent beings."[138] The triune God is perfectly "happy in Himself," yet He still "has a natural propensity and inclination to communicate happiness to some other beings [the elect]."[139] And "God created the world for His Son, that He might prepare a spouse or bride for Him to bestow His love upon; so that the mutual joys between this bride and the bridegroom are the end of creation."[140]

Some opponents of Christianity ask us why God created the universe in this place rather than in that place, and why He created the universe at this time rather than at that time. How would you respond?

JE: "There is…no difficulty in answering such questions as these: What cause was there why the universe was placed in such a part of space, and why created at such a time? For if there be no space beyond the universe [which there is not], it was impossible that the universe should be created in another place; and if there was no time before the creation [which there was not], it was impossible that it should be created at another time."[141]

Do you believe that the Bible teaches us that the earth is very young?

JE: I do. "When Christ came from heaven [at the incarnation]…it was [about] four thousand years from the beginning of time."[142]

The crowning act of creation, of course, was the creation of man, the image bearer of God. But we will get to this below.

JE: Very well.

There are some in our days who teach that we don't need God to posit the world in which we live; that the world could be self-created. How do you respond?

JE: This is irrational and impossible. "To suppose that it [the creation] is from the world itself carries a contradiction; and to suppose that it is from nothing is a contradiction."[143]

Providence

Do you also agree with the Shorter Catechism *(Q. 11) that "God's works of providence are, His most holy, wise, and powerful preserving and governing all His creatures, and all their actions"?*

JE: Yes, I do. "God determines whatsoever comes to pass, and orders all things by His providence."[144] "The constant exercise of the infinite power of God is necessary to preserve bodies in being."[145]

I believe that you see Ezekiel's wheels as symbolic of God's work of providence.

JE: That is true. And "work of providence" is really one united plan, God's "grand design," as He carries out His work in redemptive history. Nothing can change or overthrow the sovereign, providential work of God: "Hence we may see what a consistent thing divine providence is. The consideration of what has been may greatly serve to show us the consistence, order, and beauty of God's works of providence. If we behold the events of providence in any other view than that in which it has been set before us, it will all look like confusion, like a number of jumbled events coming to pass without any order or method, like the tossing of the waves of the sea. Things will look as though one confused revolution came to pass after another merely by blind chance, without any design or certain end. But if we consider the events of providence in the light in which they have been set before us under this doctrine in which the Scriptures set them before us, they appear far from being jumbled and confused, but an orderly series of events, all wisely ordered and directed in excellent harmony and consistence, tending all to one end. The wheels of providence are not turned round by blind chance, but they are full of eyes round about, as Ezekiel represents; and they are guided by the Spirit of God, where the Spirit goes they go. And all God's works of providence through all ages: they meet in one at last as so many lines meeting in one center. It is with God's work of providence as it is the work of creation: it is but one work. The events of providence be not so many distinct independent works of providence, but they are rather so many different parts of one work of providence: it is all one work, one regular scheme. God's works of providence be not disunited and jumbled, without connection or dependence. But all are united, just as the several parts of one building: there are many stones, many pieces of timber, but all are joined and fitly framed together that they make but one building. They have all but one foundation, and are united at last in one topstone."[146]

But we as men don't always see this correctly or fully, do we?

JE: No, we don't. Let me explain it this way: "God's providence may not unfitly be compared to a large and long river, having innumerable branches beginning in different regions, and at a great distance one from another, and all conspiring to one common issue. After their very diverse and contrary courses which they hold for a while, yet all gathering more and more together the nearer they come to their common end, and all at length discharging themselves at one mouth into the same ocean. The different streams of this river are ready to look like mere jumble and confusion to us because of the limitedness of our sight, whereby we can't see from one branch to another and can't see the whole at once, so as to see how all are united in one. A man that sees but one or two streams at a time can't tell what their course tends to. Their course seems very crooked, and the different streams seem to run for a while different and contrary ways. And if we view things at a distance, there seem to be innumerable obstacles and impediments in the way to hinder their ever uniting and coming to the ocean, as rocks and mountains and the like. But yet if we trace them they all unite at last and all come to the same issue, disgorging themselves in one into the same great ocean [God]. Not one of all the streams fail of coming hither at last."[147]

Technically, though, you believe in a form of continuous creation.

JE: Yes, I do. Not only did God create all things *ex nihilo* at the first, but He continues to re-create all things, thereby preserving and governing them. "It is most agreeable to the Scripture, to suppose creation to be performed new every moment. The Scripture speaks of it not only as past but as a present, remaining, continual act."[148] "Therefore the existence of created substances, in each successive moment, must be the effect of the immediate agency, will, and power of God...the existence of each created person and thing, at each moment of it, be from the immediate continued creation of God. It will certainly follow from these things, that God's preserving created things in being is perfectly equivalent to a continued creation, or to His creating those things out of nothing at each moment of their existence."[149] Or said more simply, "the universe is created out of nothing every moment...and if it were not for our imaginations, which hinder us, we might see that wonderful work performed continually."[150]

The fact of God's providential control of all things should give the Christian the greatest comfort.

JE: Exactly so, "as Mediator [Jesus Christ] rules all events...so as to conduce to the good of His church, and to bring to pass the ends of His mediation."[151] "The universe is the chariot in which God rides and makes progress towards the last end of all things on the wheels of His providence.... Therefore [Ezekiel 1:25-26] signifies as much as that God governs the whole world for the good of His church; the wheels of the chariot of the universe move for them, and the progress that God makes therein on His throne above the firmament, the pavement of His chariot, is for them, and every event in the universe is in subserviency to their help and benefit."[152]

Yet at the same time, we are not able to be led by providence alone, but by Scripture alone.

JE: That is correct. "There is a voice of God in His providence, that may be interpreted and well understood by the rule of His Word; and providence may, to our dark minds and weak faith, confirm the Word of God as it fulfills it: but to improve divine providence thus, is quite a different thing from making a rule of providence. There is a good use may be made of the events of providence, of our own observation and experience, and human histories, and the opinion of the fathers and other imminent men; but finally all must be brought to one rule, *viz.* the Word of God, and that must be regarded as our only rule."[153]

Christology

As you have already said, the Bible teaches us that the second person of the Trinity is fully divine. What about the human nature of Jesus Christ?

JE: Yes, "as Christ is one of the persons of the Trinity, He is God."[154] He "is a divine person."[155] As the eternal Son of God, "Christ is the shining forth of the Father's glory."[156] But from the time of His incarnation, Jesus Christ is also fully human; He possesses both a human body and a human soul. "He is not only in the divine nature, but in the human nature. He is truly a man, and has all possible human excellencies."[157] Not only is He "the Son of God," He is also "the Son of man. He is both God and man."[158] And being conceived in the womb of the virgin Mary "by the Holy Ghost…it is impossible that [He] should have any sin."[159] Jesus Christ is "altogether lovely," He is "chief among ten thousands." And all of the "spiritual beauty of His human nature, consisting in His meekness, lowliness, patience, heavenliness, love to God, love to men…all is summed up in His holiness." Then too, the "beauty of His divine nature, of which the beauty of His human nature is the image and reflection, does also primarily consist in His holiness."[160]

Reformed theology maintains that there is a perfect "hypostatic" union which exists between the divine nature and the human nature of Christ in one person. And in this union, both natures remain distinct. Christ is fully God and fully man, yet one Lord Jesus Christ.

JE: This doctrine is correct. "The divine *Logos* is so united to the humanity of Christ that it spoke and acted by it, and made use of its organs, as is evident by the history of Christ's life, and as it is evident He will do at the day of judgment. And this He does not occasionally once in awhile, as He may in the prophets, but constantly, not by occasional communication, but a constant and everlasting union."[161] It is also evident that "the Holy Spirit is the bond of union by which the human nature of Christ is united to the divine, so as to be one person."[162]

Does Christ continue in His human nature?

JE: Yes; when He "was born of a woman [Mary], [He] took upon Himself our nature, [He] is still in our nature, and will be forever."[163]

From what you have said, you would reject the Kenotic theory which teaches that at the incarnation Christ laid aside some or all of His divine attributes?

JE: I do reject this theory. "When the apostle [Paul] says Christ emptied Himself, as Philippians 2:7," all that he means is that "He [Christ] appeared in the world without His former glory and joy."[164] But "He did as it were divest Himself of all that manifestation of [His] glory and the appearance of the infinite Sovereign of the world. That manifestation of power and greatness which He had."[165]

It is common in the teaching of Reformed theology to say that when we worship Christ, the God-man, we do so as touching His divine nature, and not His human nature; because to worship the human nature of Christ would be a form of idolatry. Do you agree with this?

JE: Yes, I do. "Men would...fall into idolatry" if they render "worship to the human nature" of Christ.[166]

Why is Christ, the second person of the Godhead, the Mediator, rather than one of the other persons of the Trinity?

JE: "Christ, in being Mediator between the Father and the saints, may be said to be Mediator between the Father and the Holy Spirit, who acts in the saints. And therefore it was fitting that the Mediator should not be either the Father of the Spirit, but a middle person between them both."[167]

How is Jesus Christ the Logos *of God?*

JE: As we saw earlier, "the name of the second person of the Trinity [*Logos*] evidences that He is God's idea." He is both "the reason [logic] of God" and "the Word of God." And as the "inward Word" of God, He gives us "the outward Word of God," which is "Scripture."[168]

As the God-man, Jesus Christ is the paradigm for us in all things.

JE: Surely this is the case. "He was the greatest instance of ardency, vigor, and strength of love, to both God and man that ever was."[169]

In Reformed thought it is common to speak of Christ's active and passive obedience. The former has to do with His obedience to the law of God in behalf of His people, and the latter has to do with His suffering for them. Is this accurate?

JE: Yes, properly understood, it is permissible to speak in this way. "For if the Son of God is substituted in the sinner's stead, then He takes the sinner's obligations on Himself. For instance, He must take the obligations the sinner is under to perform perfect obedience to the divine law…[and] if the Son of God is substituted in the sinner's stead, then He comes under the sinner's obligation to suffer the punishment which man's sin deserved."[170] "We are justified by Christ's active obedience thus: His active obedience was one thing that God saw to be needful in order to retrieve the honor of His law, as well as His suffering [passive obedience] for the breach of it. That the eternal Son of God should subject Himself to that law which man had broken, and become obedient to it [active obedience], was what greatly honored the law and the authority that established it. So that we are saved by it [active obedience], as well as His death [passive obedience]."[171]

We distinguish between the active and passive obedience of Christ, but we do not want to separate them; is this correct?

JE: Exactly; "every act of obedience was propitiatory and every act of obedience was meritorious."[172] And "Jesus Christ kept all His Father's commandments."[173]

Was it necessary for Christ to perfectly obey the law for Himself (as touching His human nature) as well as for His people?

JE: Yes, it was. "Had not Christ perfectly" obeyed the law of God and "satisfied for the sins of men, and so done away all his imputed guilt, He could not have appeared a second time without sin [Hebrews 9:28], but must always have remained under the tokens of God's curse for sin."[174]

In Hebrews 13:8 we read that "Jesus Christ is the same yesterday, today, and forever." How is Jesus Christ unchangeable?

JE: "Christ is thus unchangeable in two respects. 1) In His divine nature. As Christ is one of the persons of the Trinity, He is God, and so has the divine nature, or the Godhead, dwelling in Him; and all the divine attributes belong to Him, of which immutability or unchangeableness is one. Christ, in His human nature, was not absolutely unchangeable…but the divine nature of Christ is absolutely unchangeable; 2) Christ is unchangeable in His office. He is unchangeable as the Mediator and Savior of His church and people."[175]

The Bible teaches that Jesus Christ lived a sinless life, but the question is often asked, was it possible for Him to have sinned?

JE: "Having the divine nature to uphold it [His human nature], it was not liable to fall and commit sin, as Adam and the fallen angels did."[176]

It is common in theological parlance to speak about the threefold offices of Christ: Prophet, Priest, and King.

JE: Yes, and this is proper. "To believe in Christ is to hearken to Him as a Prophet, to yield ourselves subject to Him as a King, and to depend upon Him as a Priest."[177]

How did Jesus Christ serve in His role as Prophet?

JE: As Prophet, Christ was "divinely instructed and sent by God to declare to men those things that are secret and not known but by divine revelation."[178] And, of course, it is by means of the Bible that "Christ communicates His light to us."[179] But we should also note that "there are two ways of representing and recommending true religion and virtue to the world; the one, by doctrine and precept; the other by instance and example.... Jesus Christ, the great Prophet of God, when He came to be 'the light of the world,' to teach and enforce true religion, in a greater degree than ever had been done before, made use of both these methods. In His doctrine He not only declared the mind and will of God, the nature and properties of that virtue which becomes creatures of our make and in our circumstances, more clearly and fully than ever it had been done before; and more powerfully enforced it by what He declared of the obligations and inducements to holiness; but He also in His own practice gave a most perfect example of the virtue He taught. He exhibited to the world such an illustrious pattern of humility, divine love, discreet zeal, self-denial, obedience, patience, resignation, fortitude, meekness, forgiveness, compassion, benevolence, and universal holiness, as neither men nor angels ever saw before."[180] At the same time, we should say that "none do submit to Christ as their teacher, but those who truly receive Him as the Prophet, to teach them by His Word and Spirit."[181]

What about the office of Priest?

JE: "It is this office of Christ in the execution of which He makes atonement for the sin of men and procures for them the favor and blessing of God."[182] But also in His office as Priest "Christ's intercession is that which will effectually secure believers from ever totally and finally falling away from grace."[183]

In His priestly work, what did Christ atone for?

JE: "He obtained the whole of the end of His suffering—a full atonement for the sins of the whole world, and the full salvation of every one of those who were given to Him [the elect] in the covenant of redemption."[184] "Christ's sufferings were equivalent to the eternal sufferings of all the elect."[185]

You then agree with the Reformed view of the limited nature of the atonement?

JE: Yes. "Universal redemption must be denied...if we acknowledge that Christ knows all things. For if Christ certainly knows all things to come, He certainly knew, when He died, that there were such and such men that would never be the better for His death. And therefore, it was impossible that He should die with an intent to make them (particular persons) happy. For it is a right-down contradiction [to say that] He died with an intent to make them happy, when at the same time He knew that they would not be happy."[186] "God gave Christ to die for the elect."[187]

What about those elect persons who lived before Christ became incarnate; were they also saved by Christ's atonement?

JE: Yes, they were. "It is manifest that all that ever obtained the pardon of their sins, from the foundation of the world till Christ came...obtained forgiveness through the sacrifice of Christ."[188]

The atonement is central, then, to biblical Christianity.

JE: "That great Christian doctrine of Christ's satisfaction, His vicarious sufferings and righteousness, by which He offered an infinite price to God for our pardon and acceptance to eternal favor and happiness...[is the] center and hinge of all doctrines of pure [biblical] revelation."[189]

Since it is impossible for God to die, Christ must have died as touching His human nature. How then could His death be of infinite value?

JE: True it is that "the divine nature cannot suffer."[190] "The divine nature is not capable of suffering, for it is impassible, and infinitely above all suffering."[191] "Indeed it was the human nature that was offered, but it was the same person with the divine, and therefore was an infinite price."[192] "The Logos felt nothing, no pain, and suffered no disgrace, but it was the human nature [that suffered]."[193]

You also teach, I believe, that the human nature of Christ was offered up as a sacrifice on the altar of His divine nature.

JE: This is so. "The altar of burnt offering was a type of the divine nature of Christ which is the altar on which Christ offered up the sacrifice of His human nature.... It was the deity of Christ that gave the infinite value and virtue to His sufferings."[194]

What affect does this priestly, mediatorial work of Christ have on the prayers of the saints?

JE: "We have a glorious Mediator who has prepared the way so that our prayers may be heard consistent with the honor of God's justice and majesty.... He has, by His blood, made atonement for our sin so that our guilt need not stand in the way as a separating wall between God and us, and that our sins might not be a cloud through which our prayers cannot pass.... Christ, by His obedience, has purchased this privilege: that the prayers of those who believe in Him should be heard. He has not only removed the obstacles to our prayers, but has merited a hearing of them.... Christ enforces the prayers of His people by His intercession at the right hand of God in heaven. He has entered for us into the holy of holies with the incense which He has provided, and there He makes continual intercession for all who come to God in His name, so that their prayers come to God the Father through His hands."[195]

This should encourage God's people to pray boldly, expecting great things from Him.

JE: Yes, it should. "God never begrudges His people anything they desire…nothing that they need, nothing that they ask of God, nothing that their desires can extend themselves to, nothing that their capacity can contain, no good that can be enjoyed by them, is so great, so excellent that God begrudges it to them…. Therefore let the godly take encouragement from hence in their prayers to come boldly to the throne of grace, and to come frequently [because God is] ready at all times to hear and to grant you whatever you desire that tends to your happiness."[196]

What about unanswered prayer?

JE: I would offer two things here. First, "it may be [that] God sees that those particular things you have asked [for] are not best for you…. For God does not withhold it as good, nor as anything that would be good at all to you, but evil." And second, it may be that the prayer was not offered with sincerity of heart: God "has not respect to a mere pretense of prayer without any real prayer…. All real and true prayer is the voice of [sincere] faith."[197]

And all of this is due to the relationship that believers have with Christ?

JE: Yes, remember that "Christ is not only the legal head of the saints. As their head, He is their representative, and their head of government, but also their vital head, their head of influence and communication, and that both of holiness and happiness."[198]

Tell us about Christ as King.

JE: As King, "Jesus Christ is the prince of life."[199] And as King, "Jesus Christ is the great Mediator and Head of the union in whom all elect creatures in heaven and earth are united to God and to one another."[200] As King, "He is higher than the kings of the earth: For He is King of kings and Lord of lords, He is higher than the heavens, and higher than the highest angels of heaven. So great is He, that all men, all kings and princes, are as worms of the dust before Him."[201]

What happened to Christ following the resurrection?

JE: Following the resurrection "Christ entered into heaven in order to the obtaining success of His purchase.... And as He ascended into heaven, God the Father did in a visible manner set Him on the throne as King of the universe. He put the angels under Him, and He subjected heaven and earth under Him, that He might govern them for the good of the people that He had died for."[202]

We know that under the Old Testament economy the kinsman redeemer (goel) *was truly a type of Christ. How is this so?*

JE: "There were four things the *goel* was to do for his kinsman unable to act for himself: 1) He was to marry the widow of the deceased kinsman [and] raise up seed to his brother, as Christ marries the elect church that was left a widow by the first Adam, the first surety, and by the law or first covenant, the first husband, having no seed (Romans 7:3-4). 2) He was to redeem the inheritance of his poor kinsman (Leviticus 25:25). So Christ redeems the inheritance which we sold. 3) He was to ransom his poor kinsman in bondage, paying the price of his redemption (Leviticus 25:47-48, 52). Thus does Christ redeem us from bondage after we have sold ourselves. 4) He was to avenge the blood of his slain kinsman on the slayer. Thus does Christ avenge our blood on Satan."[203]

Ultimately, how do we best show our respect for Jesus Christ?

JE: "The most acceptable way of showing respect to Christ is to give hearty entertainment to His Word."[204]

How do we see the Holy Spirit in the life and ministry of Christ?

JE: In many ways. "It was by the eternal Spirit that Christ offered Himself without spot to God. It was by the Holy Spirit many ways. It was by the Holy Spirit that the human nature of Christ was united to the divine Logos, from which arises the infinite value of His blood and righteousness. It was by the eternal Spirit that Christ performed righteousness. It was by the Spirit of God that Christ was perfectly holy and performed perfect righteousness. It was by the Holy Spirit not only that His obedience was perfect, but performed with such transcendent love. It was by this Spirit that His sacrifice of Himself was sanctified, being an offering to God in the pure and fervent flame of divine love, which burnt in His heart as well as in the flame of God's vindictive justice and wrath into which He was cast. And it was this that His obedience and sacrifice were offered with such love to His people that He died for, as implied a perfect union with them, whereby it was accepted for them."[205]

---

[1] Edwards, *Works* (Yale), 4:569.

[2] Cited in *Our Great and Glorious God*, 10.

[3] Edwards, *Sermon* on Psalm 89:6.

[4] Edwards, *Works* (Yale), 8:551.

[5] Edwards, *Miscellany* 182.

[6] Stephen R. Holmes, for example, incorrectly commented, "In common with Eastern Orthodox thought, Edwards was prepared to see salvation as *theosis*, being made one with God" *(God of Grace and God of Glory: An Account of the Theology of Jonathan Edwards)*, 58.

[7] Edwards, *Works* (Yale), 8:423.

[8] Edwards, *Works* (Yale), 2:298.

[9] In the *Westminster Confession of Faith*, chapter 2 studies the being of God, and chapters 3-5 study the works of God.

[10] Edwards, *Works* (Yale), 8:428-429.

[11] Edwards, *Works* (Yale), 6:381.

[12] Edwards, *Sermon* on 1 Timothy 6:15.

[13] Edwards, *Sermon* on Isaiah 6:5.

[14] Edwards, *Works* (Yale), 8:456, 461.
[15] Edwards, *Sermon* on Zechariah 11:8.
[16] Edwards, *Religious Affections*, 98.
[17] Edwards, *Works* (Yale), 8:428.
[18] Edwards, *Works* (Yale), 2:257.
[19] Edwards, *Works* (Yale), 6:363.
[20] Edwards, *A Jonathan Edwards Reader*, 257.
[21] Edwards, *Miscellany* 650.
[22] Edwards, *Sermon* on Revelation 19:2-3.
[23] Edwards, *Sermon* on Psalm 139:7-10.
[24] Edwards, *Works* (Yale), 8:369.
[25] Edwards, *Sermon* on Psalm 89:6.
[26] Edwards, "An Essay on the Trinity," *Treatise on Grace and Other Posthumously Published Writings*, edited by Paul Helm, 105.
[27] Edwards, *Miscellany* 743.
[28] Edwards, *Sermon* on 1 John 3:15.
[29] Edwards, *Works*, II:496.
[30] Edwards, *Sermon* on Daniel 4:35.
[31] Edwards, *Works* (Yale), 6:345; *Works* (Yale), 8:461-463.
[32] Edwards, *Miscellany* 880.
[33] Edwards, *Works* (Yale), 21:377.
[34] Edwards, *Works* (Yale), 1:376.
[35] Edwards, *Works* (Yale), 6:345.
[36] Edwards, *Works* (Yale), 6:363.
[37] Edwards, *Sermon* on Numbers 23:19.
[38] Edwards, *Sermon* on Psalm 111:5.
[39] Edwards, *Miscellany* 1218.
[40] Edwards, *Sermon* on Numbers 23:19.
[41] Edwards, *Works*, II:529.
[42] Cited in Don Kistler, "The Character of God," a tape series.
[43] Edwards, *Works* (Yale), 6:342.
[44] Edwards, *Works* (Yale), 6:341-342.
[45] Edwards, *Works*, I:xiii.
[46] Cited in *Our Great and Glorious God*, 174.
[47] Edwards, *Sermon* on Job 9:4.
[48] Edwards, *Sermon* on Romans 9:18.
[49] Edwards, *Sermon* on Daniel 4:35.
[50] Edwards, *Sermon* on Daniel 4:35.
[51] Edwards, *Works*, I:35-41.
[52] Edwards, *Miscellany* 194.
[53] Edwards, *Miscellany* 74.
[54] Edwards, *Sermon* on Numbers 23:19.
[55] Edwards, *Sermon* on Romans 8:29-30.
[56] Edwards, *Miscellany* 759.

[57] Edwards, *Works* (Yale), 1:239.
[58] Edwards, *Works*, I:279.
[59] Edwards, *Sermon* on Isaiah 6:3.
[60] Edwards, *Sermon* on Romans 9:18.
[61] Edwards, *Religious Affections*, 99.
[62] Edwards, *Sermon* on 2 Peter 2:14.
[63] Edwards, *Works* (Yale), 8:133.
[64] Edwards, *Works* (Yale), 2:257-258.
[65] Edwards, *A Jonathan Edwards Reader*, 291.
[66] Edwards, *Works* (Yale), 2:298, 257.
[67] Edwards, *Sermon* on Isaiah 35:8.
[68] Edwards, *Miscellany* 1205.
[69] Edwards, *Sermon* on Luke 6:35.
[70] Edwards, *Sermon* on Romans 5:10; *Sermon* on Jeremiah 31:3; *Sermon* on Philippians 4:19.
[71] Cited in *Standing in Grace*, 34.
[72] Edwards, *Miscellany* 117.
[73] Edwards, *Miscellany* 94.
[74] Edwards, *A Jonathan Edwards Reader*, 226.
[75] Cited in *Our Great and Glorious God*, 11.
[76] Edwards, *Sermon* on Mark 9:44.
[77] Edwards, *Miscellany* 779.
[78] Edwards, *Works* (Yale), 3:131.
[79] Edwards, *Sermon* on Genesis 27:39.
[80] Edwards, *Sermon* on Zechariah 11:8.
[81] Edwards, *Sermon* on Zechariah 11:8.
[82] Edwards, *Sermon* on Psalm 89:6.
[83] Edwards, *Works* (Yale), 8:518-523.
[84] Edwards, *Works* (Yale), 15:221.
[85] Edwards, *Works* (Yale), 8:530-531.
[86] Cited in *Our Great and Glorious God*, 85, 94.
[87] Edwards, *Miscellany* 362.
[88] Edwards, *Works*, I:xlvii.
[89] Edwards, *Miscellany* 182.
[90] Edwards, *Sermon* on John 15:10.
[91] Edwards, *Works* (Yale), 21:133.
[92] Edwards, *Miscellany* 402.
[93] Edwards, *Works* (Yale), 21:135.
[94] Edwards, *Miscellany* 308.
[95] Edwards, *Miscellany* 539.
[96] Edwards, *Works* (Yale), 21:133.
[97] Cited in Amy Plantinga Pauw, *The Supreme Harmony of All*, 122.
[98] Edwards, *Works* (Yale), 15:387.
[99] Edwards, *Miscellany* 94.

[100] Edwards, *Miscellany* 448.
[101] Edwards, *Miscellany* 405.
[102] Edwards, *Works* (Yale), 21:131.
[103] Edwards, *Miscellany* 1062.
[104] Cited in Gerstner, *The Rational Biblical Theology of Jonathan Edwards*, II:189.
[105] Edwards, "Treatise on Grace," Grosart, *Selections From the Unpublished Writings of Jonathan Edwards*, 49.
[106] Edwards, *Miscellany* 1062.
[107] Edwards, *Miscellany* 958.
[108] Edwards, *Sermon* on Hebrews 1:3.
[109] Cited in *Our Great and Glorious God*, 54.
[110] Edwards, *Sermon* on Matthew 11:6.
[111] Edwards, *Works*, II:527.
[112] Edwards, *Sermon* on Job 14:5.
[113] Edwards, *Sermon* on Job 14:5.
[114] Edwards, *Works*, II:527-528, 534.
[115] Cited in *Our Great and Glorious God*, 18.
[116] Edwards, *Works*, I:217.
[117] Cited in *Our Great and Glorious God*, 83.
[118] Edwards, *Works* (Yale), 3:403.
[119] Edwards, *Miscellany* 1263.
[120] Edwards, *Sermon* on Romans 9:18.
[121] Edwards, *Works* (Yale), 8:503.
[122] Edwards, *Sermon* on Matthew 13:23.
[123] Edwards, *Miscellany* 273.
[124] Edwards, *Sermon* on Matthew 11:6.
[125] Edwards, *Sermon* on Exodus 9:16.
[126] Edwards, *Works*, II:527-528.
[127] Edwards, *Works* (Yale), 6:216.
[128] Edwards, *Works* (Yale), 9:513-514.
[129] Edwards, *Works* (Yale), 18:200.
[130] Edwards, *Miscellany* 710.
[131] Edwards, *Miscellany* 508.
[132] Edwards, *Miscellany* 702.
[133] Edwards, *Miscellany* 749.
[134] Edwards, *Works*, I:102.
[135] Edwards, *Miscellany* 679.
[136] Edwards, *Miscellany* 3.
[137] Edwards, *Miscellany* 448.
[138] Edwards, *Miscellany* 332.
[139] Edwards, *Works* (Yale), 14:153.
[140] Edwards, *Miscellany* 271.

[141] Edwards, *Works* (Yale), 6:343.
[142] Edwards, *Works* (Yale), 15:82.
[143] Edwards, *Miscellany* 749.
[144] Edwards, *Sermon* on Isaiah 3:1-2.
[145] Edwards, *Works* (Yale), 6:214.
[146] Edwards, *Works* (Yale), 9:121, 519-520.
[147] Edwards, *Works* (Yale), 9:520.
[148] Edwards, *Miscellany* 346.
[149] Edwards, *A Jonathan Edwards Reader*, 240-241.
[150] Edwards, *Works* (Yale), 6:241-242.
[151] Edwards, *Miscellany* 86.
[152] Edwards, *Selections From the Unpublished Writings of Jonathan Edwards*, 99-100.
[153] Edwards, *Works* (Yale), 4:452.
[154] Edwards, *Sermon* on Hebrews 13:8.
[155] Edwards, *Sermon* on Revelation 5:5-6.
[156] Edwards, *Sermon* on Hebrews 1:3.
[157] Edwards, *Sermon* on Ephesians 3:10.
[158] Edwards, *Miscellany* 772.
[159] Edwards, *Miscellany* 386.
[160] Edwards, *Works* (Yale), 2:258-259.
[161] Edwards, *Miscellany* 738.
[162] Edwards, *Miscellany* 764b.
[163] Edwards, *Sermon* on Psalm 108:4.
[164] Edwards, *Works* (Yale), 15:186.
[165] Edwards, *Sermon* on 2 Corinthians 8:9.
[166] Edwards, *Miscellany* 242.
[167] Edwards, *Sermon* on Ephesians 3:10.
[168] Edwards, *Miscellany* 309.
[169] Edwards, *Works* (Yale), 2:111.
[170] Edwards, *Sermon* on Ephesians 3:10.
[171] Edwards, *Miscellany* 261.
[172] Edwards, *Miscellany* 845.
[173] Edwards, *Sermon* on John 15:10.
[174] Edwards, *Works* (Yale), 15:286.
[175] Edwards, *Sermon* on Hebrews 13:8.
[176] Edwards, *Sermon* on Hebrews 13:8.
[177] Edwards, *Works* (Yale), 21:422.
[178] Edwards, *Sermon* on Deuteronomy 18:18.
[179] Edwards, *Sermon* on John 8:12.
[180] Edwards (editor), *The Life and Diary of David Brainerd*, 43.
[181] Edwards, *Works* (Yale), 12:264.

[182] Edwards, *Sermon* on Psalm 110:4.
[183] Edwards, *Sermon* on Luke 22:31.
[184] Edwards, *Sermon* on Luke 22:44.
[185] Edwards, *Miscellany* 898.
[186] Edwards, *Miscellany* t.
[187] Edwards, *Sermon* on Romans 2:10.
[188] Edwards, *Miscellany* 1283.
[189] Edwards, *Works*, II:497.
[190] Edwards, *Sermon* on Ephesians 3:10.
[191] Edwards, *Works* 9:295-296.
[192] Edwards, *Sermon* on 1 Corinthians 1:29-31.
[193] Edwards, *Miscellany* 180.
[194] Cited in Gerstner, *The Rational Biblical Theology of Jonathan Edwards*, II:429.
[195] Edwards, *Sermon* on Psalm 65:2.
[196] Edwards, *Sermon* on Psalm 21:4.
[197] Edwards, *Sermon* on Psalm 21:4.
[198] Edwards, *Sermon* on Psalm 21:4.
[199] Edwards, *Sermon* on Acts 3:15.
[200] Edwards, *Sermon* on 1 Timothy 2:5.
[201] Edwards, *Sermon* on Revelation 5:5-6.
[202] Edwards, *Works* (Yale), 9:361.
[203] Edwards, *Selections From the Unpublished Writings of Jonathan Edwards*, 112-113.
[204] Edwards, *Sermon* on Luke 10:38-42.
[205] Edwards, *Works* (Yale), 15:575.

CHAPTER 6

Edwards on Angels

You have written a good deal about angels. And you have already told us that the devil is orthodox in his faith, even though he hates and abuses the faith. But what, would you say, is the purpose of the angels?

JE: The angels serve God as the "nobles and barons of the court of heaven, as dignified servants in the palace of the King of kings."[1] "The angels of heaven do praise God together."[2] Then too, "the angels of heaven, though a superior order of being, and of a more exalted nature and faculties by far than men, are yet all ministering spirits sent forth to minister to them that shall be the heirs of heaven."[3] "God makes use of the ministry of angels in affairs relating to the eternal state of mankind."[4]

When were the angels created?

JE: On the first day of creation, with the lights.[5]

How is it that some of the angels fell into sin, while others remained holy before God?

JE: They, like mankind, were originally placed under a covenant of works. And "probably the service appointed to them as the great trial of obedience, was serving Christ, or ministering to Him in His great work that He had undertaken with respect to mankind." "When Lucifer rebelled and set himself up as a head in opposition to God and Christ, and drew away a great number of angels after him, Christ, the Son of God, manifested Himself as an opposite head, and appeared graciously to dissuade and restrain by His grace the elect angels from hearkening to Satan's temptation, so that they were upheld and preserved from eternal destruction at this time of great danger by the free and distinguishing grace of Christ. Herein Christ was the Savior of the elect angels, for though He did not save them as He did elect men from the ruin they had already deserved, and were condemned to, and the miserable state they were already in, yet He saved them from eternal destruction they were in great danger of, and other wise would have fallen into with the other angels. The elect angels joined with Him, the glorious Michael, as their captain, while the other angels hearkened to Lucifer and joined with him."[6]

Do you actually mean that Christ is the Savior of the elect angels as well as elect men?

JE: Yes, "though one is innocent [angels] and the other guilty [men], the one having eternal life by a covenant of grace [men], the other by a covenant of works [angels], yet both have eternal life by His Son Jesus Christ God man, and both, though different ways, by the humiliation and sufferings of Christ; the one as the price of life [men], the other [angels] as the greatest and last trial of their steadfast and persevering obedience. Both have eternal life through different ways, by their adherence and voluntary submission, and self-dedication to Christ crucified, and He is made the Lord and King of both…for as the angels have confirmed life in and by Christ, so have the saints."[7]

What was it that caused Lucifer and the fallen angels to rebel?

JE: "It seems to me probable that the temptation of the angels, which occasioned their rebellion, was, that when God was about to create man, or had first created him, God declared His decree to the angels that one of that human nature should be His Son, His best beloved, His greatest favorite, and should be united to His eternal Son, and that He should be their Head and King, that they should be given to Him, and should worship Him, and be His servants, attendants, and ministers: and God having thus declared His great love to the race of mankind, gave the angels the charge of them as ministering spirits to men. Satan, or Lucifer, or Beelzebub, being the archangel, one of the highest of the angels, could not bear it, thought it below him, and a great debasing of him. So he conceived rebellion against the Almighty, and drew away a vast company of the heavenly host with him."[8]

Why do you suppose it was that fallen mankind were offered a Savior, whereas the fallen angels were not?

JE: "It is probable, one reason why man has the offer of a Savior and the devils never had, was because their [the devils] sin was attended with that malice and spite and haughty scornfulness, that was equivalent to the sin against the Holy Ghost."[9]

You have alluded to the fact that the angels are superior to mankind.

JE: Yes, this is so. "Man is a creature who in his nature is vastly inferior to the angels."[10] Yet, the elect "saints are made higher [than the angels] in glory in heaven forever."[11]

What is the greatest threat today of Satan and the fallen angels?

JE: We must remember that even though "the devil is orthodox in his faith, [i.e.] he believes the true scheme of doctrine," at the same time, he "oftentimes transforms himself into an angel of light."[12] Surely "the devil is a liar."[13] And "one principal means that the devil makes use of to persuade men to sin is to persuade them that they shall escape punishment."[14]

What are your beliefs concerning "demon possession?"

JE: Although there are some demon possessed men, it is important to understand that all "wicked men are the children of the devil."[15] And "wicked men are like the man [of Luke 8:26-39] possessed with devils."[16]

How powerful is Satan?

JE: He is very powerful, but God controls him. "God holds Satan on a chain," so that his power "is a limited power."[17]

It seems strange that Satan continues to frustrate and overthrow the designs of the all-powerful, all-knowing God of the Bible, even as he knows that this God's plans will not be overthrown or frustrated.

JE: "To this I say, that although the devil be exceeding crafty and subtle, yet he is one of the greatest fools and blockheads in the world."[18]

I understand also that you believe that God will fill up the room that was left vacant in heaven when the non-elect angels fell.

JE: That is correct, but I would say it this way: "What the fallen angels have done for the ruin of mankind, has only proved an occasion of mankind's being exalted into their stead and to fill up that room that was left vacant in heaven by their fall."[19]

---

[1] Edwards, *Works*, II:607.

[2] Edwards, *Sermon* on Job 38:7.

[3] Edwards, *Miscellany* 681.

[4] Edwards, *Sermon* on Matthew 13:47-50.

[5] Edwards, *Miscellany* 1336.

[6] Edwards, *Works*, II:606.

[7] Edwards, *Works*, II:615.

[8] Edwards, *Works*, II:607.

[9] Edwards, *Miscellany* 296.

[10] Edwards, *Sermon* on Psalm 8:4-5.

[11] Edwards, *Works*, II:616.

[12] Edwards, *Sermon* on James 2:19.

[13] Edwards, *Sermon* on John 8:44.

[14] Edwards, *Sermon* on Genesis 3:4.

[15] Edwards, *Sermon* on John 8:44.

[16] Edwards, *Sermon* on Luke 8:26-39.

[17] Edwards, *Sermon* on Deuteronomy 11:26.

[18] Edwards, *Miscellany* 48.

[19] Edwards, *Miscellany* 616.

CHAPTER 7

Edwards on Man

Man is the crown of God's creation, created in the image of God Himself.

JE: Yes. "In the gradation of ends among the creatures, man is the highest step."[1] Further, man was created with both a non-physical and a physical aspect; he has both a body and a soul or spirit. The image of God rests (mainly) in the non-physical element of man. Man is a rational creature, and herein distinguished from the animals. "Our souls are made in the image of God, we have understanding and will, idea and love as God has."[2] "The soul of man, being spiritual and rational, is capable of incomparably greater beauty than the body, because the soul is capable of receiving the image of God, of which the body is not."[3] "The main difference between men and beasts is, that men are capable of reflecting upon what passes in their own minds; beasts have nothing but direct consciousness."[4]

The image of God, then, lies primarily in the fact that he, like God, is a rational being?

JE: This is what I believe. "Reason" is the "noblest…most excellent…and highest" faculty in man. It "is designed by our Maker to ever rule and exalt sense, imagination, and passion, which were made to be [its] servants."[5]

In your view, God created man as His image bearer. And you teach that there is a two-fold image of God in man. Would you explain this?

JE: "As there are two kinds of attributes in God...His moral attributes...and His natural attributes...so there is a two-fold *imago Dei* in man, his moral or spiritual image, which is his holiness...and man's natural image, consisting in man's reason and understanding, his natural ability and dominion over the creatures, which is the image of God's natural ability."[6]

Does man still retain this two-fold image of God?

JE: Yes, he does. The "natural image of God" which primarily "consists [in] the faculty of reason," is not "inconsistent with itself." That is, it is now defaced due to the Fall, but it is not effaced. Man still remains man. The moral image, however, was eradicated by the Fall, and can only be restored through the grace of God in Jesus Christ. It is here that "wicked [fallen] men are inconsistent with themselves."[7] It is here "that they are entirely under the dominion of sin."[8]

---

[1] Edwards, *Miscellany* 103.

[2] Cited in Scheick, *The Writings of Jonathan Edwards*, 136.

[3] Edwards, *Sermon* on Romans 2:10; *Sermon* on Matthew 23:27.

[4] Edwards, *Works* (Yale), 6:374.

[5] Cited in Gerald R. McDermott, *Jonathan Edwards Confronts the Gods*, 56.

[6] Edwards, *Works* (Yale), 2:256.

[7] Edwards, *Sermon* on Matthew 11:16-19.

[8] Edwards, *Sermon* on Romans 7:14.

CHAPTER 8

Edwards on Soteriology

When we discuss the matter of soteriology, we are talking about the doctrine of salvation. The Scriptures attribute salvation to the grace of God, i.e., salvation is of the Lord (Jonah 2:9; Psalm 3:8).

JE: Yes, "it is manifest that the Scripture supposes that if ever men are turned from sin, God must undertake it and He must be the doer of it, and that His doing must determine the matter; that all that others can do will [be] nothing without, and never will determine the point."[1] "God is glorified in the work of redemption in that there appears in it so absolute and universal a dependence of the redeemed on Him."[2]

Certainly this does not mean that man does not have a responsibility in the working of efficacious grace?

JE: Not at all. "In efficacious grace we are not merely passive, nor yet does God do some and we do the rest. But God does all, and we do all. God produces all, and we act all. For that is what He produces, *viz.* our own acts. God is the only proper author and fountain; we are only the proper actors. We are, in different respects, wholly passive and wholly active."[3]

And all three members of the Trinity are involved in this great work of salvation; but which person has the greatest share of this work?

JE: "Now I think it can hardly be said which of the persons in the Trinity has the greatest share in this work of redemption; it's from all of them."[4]

You have already told us that when God created Adam, He entered into a covenant of works with him, wherein Adam acted as the federal head or representative of the entire human race. In this covenant, God promised eternal life to Adam, and his posterity, upon the condition of Adam's perfect, personal obedience to God's commands. Adam, however, disobeyed God. And when he fell, all mankind (with the exception of Christ) fell with him.

JE: This is precisely so.

The Westminster Shorter Catechism *(Q. 17, 19) teaches that the Fall of Adam in the Garden of Eden "brought mankind into an estate of sin and misery." "All mankind by their fall lost communion with God, are under His wrath and curse, and so made liable to all miseries in this life, to death itself, and to the pains of hell forever." What are your comments on this?*

JE: This teaching is correct. "The beginning of the posterity of our first parents was after the Fall, for all his [Adam's] posterity by ordinary generation are partakers of the Fall and the corruption of nature that followed from it."[5] Man now "stands in absolute need of a Redeemer."[6]

Reformed theology frequently refers to fallen man's state as one of "total depravity." He is unable to do anything that pleases God.

JE: Correct. "The nature of man is so corrupted that he is become a very evil and hurtful creature."[7] The "hearts of natural men are wholly corrupt, entirely destitute of anything spiritually good, not having the least spark of love to God."[8] Men are "polluted with sin; every step they take is attended with sin, so all the works that they do are polluted. They can perform no service, no business, but they contract their guilt and defilement, that they need the renewed washing of the blood of Christ."[9]

What about the person who claims that he is not guilty of sin against God because God made him the way he is, and that he is therefore addicted to his sin, and has an excuse?

JE: "Men's being so addicted to any wicked practice that

they can't leave it is no excuse to them, but an aggravation.... There is never any overt act of sin whatever but what is voluntary." Therefore, "let not those who are addicted to wicked practices of any kind plead as an excuse for themselves that they can't leave it."[10]

How is it possible that Adam, in his pristine state, could choose to do evil?

JE: The answer lies in this: "Adam...failed in his work, because he was a mere creature, and so a mutable being. Though he had so great a trust committed to him, as the care of the eternal welfare of all his posterity, yet, not being unchangeable, he failed, and transgressed God's holy covenant."[11] "God gave our first parents [Adam and Eve] sufficient grace, though He withheld efficacious grace or a grace that should certainly uphold him in all temptations he could meet with."[12] God "only withheld His confirming grace."[13]

How is it that all mankind was affected by Adam's fall?

JE: "By virtue of the full consent of the hearts of Adam's posterity to that first apostasy...the sin of apostasy is not theirs, merely because God imputes it to them; but it is truly and properly theirs, and on that ground God imputes it to them." That is to say that Adam's posterity was "really" there with him in the Garden of Eden; and they sinned as "really" as he did. There is "a constituted union of the branches with the root." "God, in each step of proceeding with Adam, in relation to the covenant [of works]...established with him, looked on his posterity as being one with him.... And though He dealt more immediately with Adam, yet it was as the head of the whole body, and the root of the whole tree.... From which it will follow, that both the guilt...and also depravity of heart, came upon Adam's posterity just as they came upon him, as much as if he and they had all co-existed, like a tree with many branches."[14] So,

"Adam's posterity were as much concerned in the covenant of works as he himself."[15]

Is it not true that the entirety of creation was affected by the Fall?

JE: Oh yes, "this visible world has now for many ages been subjected to sin, and made as it were a servant to it.... It is a bondage the creature is subject to, from which it was partly delivered when Christ came and the gospel was promulgated in the world; and will be more fully delivered at the commencement of the glorious day we are speaking of [the millennium]; and perfectly at the day of judgment."[16]

Would you be in agreement with the traditional view that Adam represented the whole of humanity (except Christ)?

JE: Yes, Adam was our "representative who stood in our room."[17] But Christ "was not reckoned in the covenant that God made with Adam."[18]

How is it that Christ could be born of a fallen human being, and not be tainted with sin?

JE: "Christ, although He was conceived in the womb of one of fallen mankind, yet He was conceived without sin; because He was conceived by the Holy Ghost, which is divine love and holiness itself. That which infinite holiness and love immediately forms, it is impossible that it should have any sin."[19]

How does this doctrine apply to children? Many persons today consider newborn children to be innocent.

JE: "As innocent as children seem to us, yet if they are out of Christ, they are not so [innocent] in God's sight, but are young vipers, and are infinitely more hateful than young vipers."[20] "Infants...are by nature children of wrath."[21]

Is the non-believer able to do any good works?

JE: No, he is not. "There is no good work before conversion.... Seeming virtues and good works before [conversion], are not so indeed; they are a spurious brood, being bastards and not children."[22] "It would be much more absurd to suppose that such a state of nature is not bad, under a notion of men doing more honest and kind things than evil ones; than to say, the state of that ship is good, for crossing the Atlantic Ocean, though such as cannot hold together through the voyage, but will infallibly founder and sink, under a notion that it may probably go a great part of the way before it sinks, or that it will proceed and sail above water more hours than it will be in sinking"; or to insist "that the domestic [servant] of a prince was not a bad servant, because though sometimes he contemned and affronted his master to a great degree, yet he did not spit in his master's face so often as he performed acts of service."[23] The "seeming virtues and good works" of the unregenerate are nothing more than "splendid sins."[24] Even "if men be very useful in temporal things to their families, or greatly promote the temporal interest of the neighborhood, or of the public; yet if no glory be brought to God by it they are altogether useless."[25]

Does this not also apply to the non-believer's outward "love" toward his fellow man, i.e., his philanthropic deeds?

JE: Yes, it does. "If duties toward men are to be accepted by God as a part of religion and the service of the divine Being, they must be performed not only with a hearty love for men, but that love must flow from regard to Him [God]."[26]

What is the worst of all sins?

JE: "Pride is the worst viper that is in the heart, the greatest disturber of the soul's peace and sweet communion with Christ; it was the first sin that ever was, and lies lowest in the foundation of Satan's whole building…[it] is the most hidden, secret and deceitful of lusts, and often creeps in, insensibly, into the midst of religion and sometimes under the disguise of humility."[27]

What is the root of all sin?

JE: "The predominancy of self-love is the foundation of all sin."[28]

What is the root of idolatry?

JE: "There are no other idols but self and the world; but all that is positive in the corruption of heart is man's regard to idols. The great contest for the heart of man is between the true God and idols."[29]

What about the unpardonable sin, i.e., blasphemy of the Holy Spirit? What is it?

JE: "It seems to me by the Scripture, that the sin against the Holy Spirit is this: for a man, when convinced in conscience, to set himself with a free and full will to reproach, or otherwise openly and contumaciously to malign the Holy Ghost in His office, or with respect to His gracious operations…and he must do it without restraint."[30] At the same time, "he that commits this sin is guilty of reproaching all the persons of the Trinity in their work and office, for the Holy Spirit is the last of them and He by whom both the others act.… He that reproaches the Holy Ghost reproaches each person of the Trinity in their work."[31]

From what you have stated, it appears that it involves a knowledge of what is taking place.

JE: Exactly so. "Hence Christ prays that the Father would forgive those who crucified Him, because they knew not what they did [Luke 23:34]; signifying that otherwise there would be no forgiveness.… So the apostle [Paul], in what he is declaring how he persecuted the saints, says he 'obtained mercy,' because he did it in ignorance and unbelief (1 Timothy 1:13); intimating that if he had done it knowingly there would have been no mercy for him."[32]

You have also told us that immediately following the Fall of man, God entered into another covenant with elect man: the covenant of grace, which covenant itself is founded upon the supra-temporal, intra-Trinitarian covenant of redemption. In the covenant of grace, Christ, as the federal head of God's elect, fulfilled the covenant of works in their behalf, and merited their salvation. Furthermore, there is only one covenant of grace for all ages.

JE: Again, this is correct.[33] Jesus Christ "was subject to and obeyed the same [law] that Adam was subject to and was to have obeyed."[34] "What Christ did was to fulfill the covenant of works."[35] And due to this, as I have said, salvation is the same for those under the Old Testament administration as it is under the New. Both Testaments have "the same salvation," "the same Mediator" (Jesus Christ), and the same method of justification by grace alone, through faith alone, in Christ alone. The two covenants "differ only in manner and circumstances."[36]

Old Testament believers, then, were also saved by believing in Christ, just as are their New Testament counterparts.

JE: Yes, these Old Testament believers were all aware that "the Messiah was the Son of God."[37] "The whole book, both Old Testament and New, is filled up with the gospel, only with this difference, that the Old Testament contains the gospel under a veil, but the New contains it unveiled, so that we may see the glory of the Lord with open face."[38] Jesus Christ is "the Savior of the saints in all ages from the beginning of the world."[39] "It is most certain, both from Scripture and reason [according to Scripture], that there must be a reception of Christ with the faculties of the soul in order to salvation by Him, and that in this reception there is a believing of what we are taught in the gospel concerning Him and salvation by Him, and that it must be a consent of the will or an agreeableness between the disposition of the soul and those doctrines."[40] Therefore, "the religion of the church of Israel was essentially the same religion with that of the Christian church," both being "built on the holy Scriptures."[41]

From what you have told us, you would definitely be a Christian exclusivist. You believe that Jesus Christ is the only Savior, and that it is essential for one to believe in Him in order to be saved.

JE: That is clearly my view. "None but those that do live under the calls of the gospel shall be saved.... That is God's way and His only way of bringing men to salvation."[42] "A sinner is not justified before God except through the righteousness of Christ obtained by faith."[43] "It is the gospel [of Jesus Christ], and that only, that has actually been the means to bring the world to the knowledge of the true God."[44] Even under the shadows of the Old Testament, it was always "the second person of the Trinity" who appeared to His people. And those who were saved put their trust in Him.[45] Christ is "the Savior of the saints in ages from the beginning of the world."[46] God "will have no pity or mercy towards those without an interest in Christ."[47]

Are you saying that whenever God appeared in the Old Testament it was the second person of the Godhead?

JE: "It is with good reason judged that whenever God appeared in human shape that it was the second person in the Trinity, because God treats with fallen man only by this second person, who is the Mediator, and because God is always wont to reveal Himself by His Son."[48] Christ is that "person of the Trinity who has all along manifested Himself, by visible tokens of His presence in the antediluvians, the patriarchs, and the Israelites."[49]

The Old Testament believers did not know as much about Christ as do the New Testament believers; correct?

JE: True, but they knew Christ, even under the name of the "Angel of the Lord" or the "Messenger of the covenant."[50] And they knew that the coming Messiah was a "divine person...who was afterwards to come into the world and make an end of sin by offering a sacrifice that should be truly propitiatory, and that this sacrifice was that of His own blood."[51]

I believe that, along with Clement of Alexandria, Origen, Eusebius, and Augustine, you adhere to the teaching of the prisca theologia, *i.e., that the Christian religion has from the beginning of time been propagated to the heathen by God's people.*

JE: Yes, the "heathens had what they had of truth in divine things by tradition from the first fathers of nations or from the Jews."[52] "The knowledge of true religion was for some time kept up in the world by tradition.... About Moses' time, when the truth, that had been upheld by tradition, was very much lost.... God took care that there might be something new [special revelation], [which] should be very public, and of great fame, and much taken notice of abroad, in the world heard, that might be sufficient to lead sincere inquirers to the true God.... That one design of [God's] providence in these things was that the heathen nations might hear the fame of the God of Israel, and so have opportunity to come to the knowledge of Him, is confirmed by 1 Kings 8:41-43."[53] Therefore, even those in foreign lands who were saved, were saved by believing in the Christ they had heard of through the special revelation brought to them by the people of God. Even men like "Cornelius [Acts 10-11] did already in some respect believe in Christ even in the manner that the Old Testament saints were wont to do."[54]

You are fond of saying that the salvation of the elect ultimately begins in God's eternal plan.

JE: This is true. God, for His own glory and according to His own good purposes, eternally decrees the election of some and the reprobation of others: "God does exercise His sovereignty in the affair of men's eternal salvation."[55] Salvation, from beginning to end, is fully based on "the divine initiative."[56] "The things which God does for the salvation and blessedness of the saints are like an inviolable chain";[57] "God is the sole author of salvation of those that are saved even from the very first beginning of it in the eternal covenant of redemption even to the end and consummation of it in the eternal glory of the saints."[58]

The Order of Salvation

In theological circles, the word "soteriology" (from the Greek soter, *savior) is the study of the work of redemption accomplished by Jesus Christ, as it is applied to the elect. Although all three members of the Trinity are involved in the salvation of the elect, it is the Holy Spirit who applies this grace. How do you see this?*

JE: This is a proper way of stating it. The Father elects; the Son redeems those whom the Father elects; and the Spirit applies Christ's redemptive work to the elect.[59] "The Father appoints and provides the Redeemer, and accepts the price of redemption. The Son is the Redeemer and the price. He redeems by offering up Himself. The Holy Ghost immediately communicates to us the thing purchased. Yea, and He is the good purchased."[60] "God has provided a Savior for us and Christ has come and died." But "the application of the redemption of the gospel [is] by the Holy Spirit [and] is of mere grace."[61] That is, "the work of the Holy Ghost as Christ's messenger is to convince men of sin, of righteousness, and of judgment."[62] In fact, we may even say that the "Holy Spirit is the sum of all that Christ purchased for man (Galatians 3:13-14).... [He] is the vital sap which the creatures derive from the true vine [Jesus Christ].... So that true, saving grace is no other than that very love of God, that is, God, in one of the persons of the Trinity [the Holy Spirit], uniting Himself to the soul of a creature as a vital principle, dwelling there and exerting Himself by the faculties of the soul of man, in His own proper nature, after the manner of a principle of nature."[63]

You have spoken of "saving grace" here. Tell us, please, the difference between what is sometimes referred to as "common grace" and this "saving grace."

JE: "Such phrases as common grace, and special or saving grace, may be understood as signifying either diverse kinds of influence of God's Spirit on the hearts of men, or diverse fruits and effects of that influence.... So sometimes the phrase common grace is used to signify that kind of action or influence of the Spirit of God to which are owing those religious or moral attainments that are common to both saints and sinners, and so signifies as much as common assistance; and sometimes those moral or religious attainments themselves that are the fruits of this assistance are intended. So likewise the phrase special or saving grace is sometimes used to signify that particular kind or degree of separation or influence of God's Spirit, when saving actions and attainments arise in the godly."[64]

Is common grace ever withdrawn?

JE: Yes, in hell God will withdraw His common grace from the damned, and they will be "deprived forever of all good."[65]

I believe it is your view that the salvation of the elect (both Old and New Testaments) has to do with their relationship with Christ. He is the federal head of His elect people; He is their representative, and they are in union with Him.

JE: This is the biblical view, and this union is foundational to the entirety of the order of salvation. It is "this relation or union to Christ, whereby Christians are said to be in Christ...is the ground of their right to His benefits."[66] "God the Father makes no covenant and enters into no treaty with fallen man distinctly by themselves. He will transact with them in such a friendly way no other way than by and in [union with] Christ Jesus as members and as it were parts of Him."[67] In saving faith there is "such a kind of union as there [is] between a head and living members, between stock and branches...there is an entire, immediate, perpetual dependence for and derivation of nourishment, refreshment, beauty, fruitfulness, and all supplies, yea, life and being."[68] That is, by God's "constitution...Christ is made the root of the tree, whose branches are His spiritual seed and He is the head of the new creation."[69] Moreover, "by virtue of the believer's union with Christ, he does really possess all things.... I'll tell you what I mean by possessing all things. I mean that God, three in one, all that He is, and all that He has, and all that He does, all that He has made or done, the whole universe, bodies and spirits, light, heaven, angels, men and devils, sun, moon, stars, land, sea, fish, fowls, all the silver and gold, kings and potentates, as well as mere men, are as much the Christian's as the money in his pocket, the clothes he wears, or the house he dwells in, as the victuals he eats; yea, more properly his, more advantageously, more his than if he commands all those things mentioned to be just in all respects as he pleased, at any time, by virtue of the union with Christ, because Christ who certainly does thus possess all things is entirely his, so that he possesses it all...only he has not the trouble of managing of it but Christ to whom it is no trouble, manages it for him, a thousand times as much as to his advantage as he could himself, if he had the managing of all.... And who would desire to possess all things more than to have all things managed just according to his will."[70]

And what is it that brings about this union?

JE: "Faith is the...uniting act of the soul towards Jesus Christ whereby it receives and closes with Him."[71]

In this union with Christ, however, believers do not become in any sense deified.

JE: No, Christians are not "made partakers of the essence of God, and so are not 'Godded' with God, and 'Christed' with Christ, according to the abominable and blasphemous language and notions of some heretics...but they are partakers of God's fullness...that is, of God's spiritual beauty and happiness, according to the capacity of a creature."[72]

Reformed theology teaches that there is a logical order (called the ordo salutis*) which God has ordained, by which the application of* *redemption is applied to the elect, as well as the means thereunto. That is, salvation is not to be seen as a one step event. One is not converted and immediately glorified. Rather, there is a process involved. But even as we study the process, we must keep in mind that some of the parts of the* ordo salutis *may be synchronous, and the parts can in no way be separated.*

JE: This is well stated. They are like "strings in concert, if one is struck others sound with it."[73] "Man's soul was ruined by the Fall.... The design was to restore the soul of man in conversion...and to carry on the restoration in sanctification, and to perfect in glory."[74]

Please tell us about this order of salvation.

JE: Okay, I will.

Universal call

JE: First, there is a "universal call" which goes out to all men who come under the hearing of the Word of God preached. This general call is "to sinners universally," inviting them to come to Christ for their salvation.[75] We have already seen that without the Word of God, there is no salvation possible. The "heathen" cannot be converted without it.[76] Only those who come "under the call of the gospel" can be saved.[77] Hence, when there is a "famine" of the Word of God in a land, it is a disastrous thing, and a sign of God's judgment.[78]

Now you have already said that you adopt the Calvinistic teaching that man, prior to regeneration, is in a state of total depravity, unable to do anything that pleases God.

JE: Yes, man "stands in absolute need of a Redeemer."[79]

And as you have also said, we know that the only way man can come to know about this Redeemer is through the gospel. We know that when the Word of God is preached, many persons do not heed it. Some hearers are hardened by it, and reject it outright. Others are convicted of their sin by the gospel message and are "awakened" to their desperate state.

JE: Yes, "it is always the effect of God's Word, either to harden or to soften. It opens the eyes of some, and turns them from darkness unto light. The eyes of others are closed by it.... The light of the gospel enlightens some, and others it strikes blind."[80] But you are also correct that some hearers "are first awakened with a sense of their miserable condition by nature, the danger they are in of perishing eternally, and that it is of great importance to them that they speedily...get into a better state."[81]

Still, however, these "awakened" sinners have not yet responded to the universal call of the gospel. What are they able to do?

JE: They must seek their salvation.

We know that the Puritans are well known for their development of the doctrine of "seeking salvation." Your later student John Gerstner said, however, that you developed it most thoroughly. What is this doctrine about?

JE: "God directs us in His Word to the work of seeking salvation in a way of constant observance of all duty. If we would be saved, we must seek salvation, for although men do not obtain heaven of themselves, yet they do not go there accidentally, or without any intention or endeavors of their own. God, in His Word, has directed men to seek their salvation if they hope to obtain it."[82]

Let me see if I understand this correctly. You believe that apart from the grace of God, fallen man will perish in his sin. But as Dr. Gerstner explained it, you teach that even though he has no spiritual ability to "close with Christ," the "awakened" sinner, being under conviction, being aware of his spiritual condition, and being concerned about it, does have the natural ability to do those things which may indeed lead to his salvation. That is, whereas only the regenerate man has the spiritual ability to "seek" God, the unregen-

erate man still has the natural ability to do so. The unregenerate man can and should go to church, where he will hear the gospel preached. He can and should read the Bible. He can and should cry out to God for mercy. He can and should talk to his pastor and other Christians about his need for a Savior, asking them to also pray for his salvation. None of these acts of "seeking" will merit the lost sinner anything before God. But God may use these to draw the sinner savingly to Christ. Is this correct?

JE: Basically, yes. "It is true [that] men never will be disposed to use the means [of grace] unless they are awakened...but that does not argue that the using the means is not in their [natural] power."[83] The "seeking sinner" must realize that "persons ought to do what they can for their salvation."[84] They must know that "God stands ready to forgive every sinner upon his hearty confessing and forsaking sin."[85] And "if we truly come to God for mercy the greatness of our sin will be no impediment to pardon."[86] To be sure, God does not "make any promises of success to unregenerated seekers of salvation."[87] Yet, there is a "greater probability" that those "who seek" their salvation will indeed be converted, because "we know that God's manner is to bestow His grace on men by outwards means; otherwise, to what purpose is the Bible, and sabbath, and preaching, and sacraments, or doctrinal knowledge of religion?"[88] For certain, "a possibility of being saved is much to be preferred to a certainty of perishing."[89]

It seems that you disagree here with some of the other Puritans who taught a form of "preparation" wherein there are certain steps which a person must pass through in order to be saved.

JE: You are correct, I disagree with this teaching. It is "unscriptural" to insist on "a particular account of the distinct method and steps" involved in salvation.[90] Early on in my life I wrote "the chief thing, that now makes me in any measure to question my own good estate, is my not having experienced in those particular steps, wherein the people of New England, and anciently the Dissenters of Old England, used to experience it."[91] I believe that "there is an endless variety in the particular manner and circumstances in which persons are wrought on [savingly brought to Christ]."[92]

What would be some of the stumbling blocks to those seeking salvation?

JE: "So oftentimes sinners, when they begin to seek salvation, keep back something that is dear and tender in their eyes, and flatter themselves that they are not obliged to deliver it up...but God will surely look upon them as enemies till all is delivered up and nothing kept back."[93]

Isn't there a vast distinction between true seekers and non-believing seekers?

JE: Oh yes; "true seekers [are] those who seek from love and [a] sense of the value of [the] thing sought, and with longing desire after the thing for its own sake." "Natural men," on the other hand, "seek only from fear and self-love."[94]

How does one know if the convictions he is under are coming from the Holy Spirit rather than from the evil one?

JE: "Whatsoever convictions and awakenings are agreeable to the truth, [that is], they are according to the Word of God," then they are from the Holy Spirit. He is the author of "real conviction of the truth of the gospel."[95]

Effectual Call

JE: So, the universal call is not efficacious. It is only when the Holy Spirit applies the Word to the elect sinner's heart that the call of God becomes "effectual." "Whatever in the work of redemption is done immediately or upon men's souls is the work of the Spirit." And "the work of the Holy Ghost [is] to make men understand the way of sinners' reconciliation and acceptance with God through Christ." He is the one who gives "divine light" "into the heart of converts."[96] "This spiritual light is not the suggestion of any new truths, or propositions not contained in the Word of God." Rather, the Spirit "gives a due apprehension of those truths that are taught in the Word of God."[97] "The first act of the Spirit of God is in spiritual understanding or in the sense of the mind, its perception of glory and excellency, etc.—in the ideas it has of divine things."[98]

Regeneration

JE: Although regeneration and effectual calling stand in the closest possible relationship, there is a difference in the two. Regeneration is the work of the Holy Spirit, as a result of the effectual call, wherein He prepares the heart of the elect sinner to respond to the call of God. "Except a man be born again he cannot see the kingdom of God."[99] This work of "divine assistance" is always "efficacious." It is "irresistible grace."[100] "If ever men are turned from sin, God must undertake it; that it is His doing that must determine the matter; that all that others can do, will avail nothing, without His agency."[101] The work of the Holy Spirit in the new birth is "internal" and "supernatural." "It is no wonder that Christ said that we must be born again."[102] "It is the Spirit of Christ that is the immediate teacher and instructor to give a true sight of Christ.... These things are done by the Spirit of Christ alone."[103]

So in regeneration, the "spiritual appetite" that was lost in the Fall is restored?

JE: Yes. "By the Fall, the spiritual appetite was lost.... In regeneration, the spiritual appetite is again, in some measure, restored.... He that is truly born again hungers and thirst after righteousness. It is his meat and drink to do the will of his Father which is in heaven."[104] "The first effect of the power of God in the heart in regeneration, is to give the heart a divine taste or sense; to cause it to have a relish of the loveliness and sweetness of the supreme excellency of the divine nature."[105]

There are some who deny that the grace of God you are speaking of here is irresistible. How would you respond?

JE: "To dispute…whether divine assistance is always efficacious or no, is perfectly ridiculous. For it is self-evident that the divine assistance is always efficacious to do that which we are assisted to; that is, it is always efficacious to that which it is efficacious to."[106]

Conversion

We are aware that you sometimes use the terms effectual calling, conversion, repentance, and regeneration as approximately synonymous terms. But you also distinguish them. We also know that you believe that regeneration results in conversion, in which the elect sinner is brought into a filial and intimate relationship with God, through Christ.

JE: Yes, "there is such a thing as conversion."[107] And this "work of conversion is a great affect of God's power and grace in the heart."[108]

What is it that actually "assures" the heart of the elect sinner in this matter of conversion?

JE: I would say "that seeing of the glory of Christ is what tends to assure the heart of the truth of the gospel."[109]

And this work of conversion is the work of God the Spirit; correct?

JE: Yes, "it is the work of the Spirit of Christ only to give a true sight of Christ." "Hence we learn that the prime alteration that is made in conversion, that which is first and the foundation of all, is the alteration of the temper and disposition and spirit of the mind; for what is done in conversion is nothing but conferring the Spirit of God, which dwells in the soul and becomes there a principle of life and action."[110]

How is the Word of God used in this work of conversion?

JE: "It is not intended that outward means have no concern in this affair…. The mind cannot see the excellency of any doctrine, unless that doctrine be first in the mind; but the seeing of the excellency of the doctrine may be immediately from the Spirit of God; though the conveying of the doctrine or proposition itself may be by the Word [of God]."[111] Scripture is "the instrument which God makes use [of] to reveal the beauty of Christ unto the soul."[112]

When you speak of "seeing the glory of Christ," and having a "true sight of Christ," you are not talking about some mystical experience.

JE: Definitely not; this kind of "seeing" "consists in the inward sense of the heart…[which will] convince you of the truth of the gospel…. [And] if you have had a true sight of Christ it will make your heart rest in Him as Savior."[113]

In Reformed theology it is generally considered to be the case that in conversion, the Holy Spirit graciously acts upon the regenerated individual, causing him to respond to the effectual call in faith and repentance. Is this also your view?

JE: Yes, it is fair to say that faith and repentance, although separate acts, are so closely related that they cannot be temporally separated: "So saving repentance and faith are implied in one another. They are both one conversion of the soul from sin to God through Christ."[114] "Repentance is often spoken of as the special condition of remission of sins," and "remission of sins is by faith in Jesus Christ," so "that faith and repentance are not to be looked upon as properly two distinct things"; rather, we should recognize "that evangelical repentance is a certain exercise of faith in Jesus Christ."[115] Or said another way, "repentance is implied in faith."[116]

As you are well aware, the Greek word for "repentance" (metanoia)*, has to do with a "change of mind." Would you speak to this, please?*

JE: You are correct in saying that repentance "signifies a change of the mind." In genuine repentance there is "a change or turning from sin to God." "The change of mind in repentance is that in which saving faith is attained."[117]

According to the Westminster Shorter Catechism *(Q. 87), a truly repentant sinner recognizes himself as an egregious sinner in the eyes of God. Perhaps this is what Paul is speaking about in 1 Timothy 1:15, where he refers to himself as the worst of sinners. Isn't there a sense in which a converted person should see himself as the same?*

JE: Absolutely so: "It has often appeared unto me, that if God should mark iniquity against me, I should appear the very worst of all mankind; of all that have been, since the beginning of the world to this time; and that I should have by far the lowest place in hell."[118] My young friend, the missionary David Brainerd, spoke in a similar way. In his diary he wrote: "No poor creature stands in need of divine grace more than I, and none abuse more than I have done, and still do.... I am full of sin."[119]

Do you also agree with the Shorter Catechism *(Q. 86) definition of saving faith: "Faith in Jesus Christ is a saving grace, whereby we receive and rest upon Him alone for salvation, as He is offered to us in the gospel?"*

JE: I do. "Faith is the soul's embracing and acquiescing in the revelation the Word of God gives us of Jesus Christ as our Savior."[120] "The definition [of saving faith] might have been expressed in these words: faith is the soul's entirely adhering and acquiescing in the revelation of Jesus Christ as our Savior—Or thus: faith is the soul's embracing that truth of God, that reveals Jesus Christ as our Savior—Or thus: faith is the soul's entirely acquiescing in, and depending upon, the truth of God, revealing Christ as our Savior."[121]

By this statement I assume that you would oppose the teaching that one can have Christ as Savior, but not as Lord?

JE: You are correct. "Justifying faith" necessitates "receiving Christ in all His offices—and so in the office of King" as well as in the others. "There is in justifying faith...a holiness of taste and nature, a conformity of the heart and consent of the inclination to the holiness of God [the Father] and Christ, and to God's revealed will [Scripture]."[122]

You have said, though, that there are various kinds of non-justifying faith spoken of in the Bible. Only one kind of faith is justifying faith.

JE: True. The kind of spurious faith which "rises only from superficial impressions is wont to whither away for want of root when it comes to be tried by the difficulties of religion."[123]

Let's talk about saving faith for a bit. What is it, and what is it not?

JE: "Saving faith differs from all common faith in its nature, kind, and essence."[124] "A true faith includes more than a mere belief; it is accepting the gospel, and includes all acceptance.... It is something more than a mere assent of the understanding, because it is called obeying the gospel.... This expression of obeying the gospel seems to denote the heart's yielding to the gospel in what it proposes to us in its call. The best, clearest, and most perfect definition of justifying faith (and most according to the Scripture) is this: faith is our soul's entirely embracing the revelation of Jesus Christ as our Savior...faith is the soul's entirely acquiescing in and depending upon the truth of God, revealing Christ as our Savior. It is the whole soul according and assenting to the truth and embracing it."[125]

And you also believe that this faith is a gift of God?

JE: It is. "It is God that gives us faith whereby we close with Christ."[126]

What things would you say are essential for a sinner to come to a saving knowledge of God through Jesus Christ?

JE: "There are these three things necessary: (1) to see our danger of eternal misery, (2) to see the absolute necessity of a savior, and (3) to see the sufficiency and excellency of the Savior [Jesus Christ] that is offered. The first is given in conviction, the second in humiliation, the third in conversion."[127]

It is common in Reformed circles to say that genuine faith involves knowledge, assent, and trust.[128] *It is not enough to know the truth about Jesus Christ as presented in the gospel; nor is it sufficient to understand the message and merely assent to it in verbal agreement, as essential as these are. This seems to be your view as well. Is this true?*

JE: Yes, it is. Saving faith "is the whole soul's active agreeing, according, and symphonizing with this truth." It is an "adhering to the truth, and acquiescing in it."[129] "Faith is a uniting with Christ, not a mere recognition of His existence."[130] It involves "an embracing the promises of God, and fiducial relying on them, through Christ for salvation."[131] "There is a difference between having a rational judgment that honey is sweet, and having a sense [taste] of its sweetness." The same is true with regard to saving faith: There is "a true sense of the divine and superlative excellency of the things of religion; a real sense of the excellency of God and Jesus Christ, and of the work of redemption, and the ways and works of God." There is "a true sense of the divine excellency of the things of God's Word [which] does more directly and immediately convince us of their truth." When one has this "sense," he acquiesces to the "light of the glorious gospel of Christ." And he does so because "God has infused such a lively apprehension into the minds of the godly of divine things, as if they had tasted." The saint, therefore, "does not merely rationally believe that God is glorious, but he has a sense of the gloriousness in his heart."[132]

In the Westminster Confession of Faith *(14:2) we read that saving faith entails believing "to be true whatsoever is revealed in the Word [of God], for the authority of God Himself speaks therein." Do you agree with this statement?*

JE: I do, indeed; "the divine authority of the Scriptures is one of the [necessary] articles" of a genuine faith.[133]

At his conversion the elect child of God has new desires, new habits, infused into him by the Spirit; correct?

JE: Correct. When a man "is changed from a sinner to a saint he has new principles of perception and action; principles that are entirely diverse and not arising merely from [a] new disposition of the old or contracted habits as those changes that are wrought by education do. They are principles that are vastly superior to those he had before."[134] The new nature of man is "wrought in the heart wholly by the Spirit," and it "dwells in the hearts of the saints...as an inward, ardent, powerful principle of operation."[135] This change affects the whole man.[136] God becomes his "best portion." He now "prefers God before all other things, either in heaven or on earth."[137]

Could you explain this further, please?

JE: What this means is that the Spirit "unites Himself with the mind of the saint...as a new supernatural principle of life and action."[138] In fact, there is a sense in which we may even say that the Holy Spirit is the new principle Himself: "The Holy Spirit or the third person of the Trinity in His operations and fruits is the sum of the blessings that Christ purchased for us in the work of our redemption."[139] Herein consists true virtue.

In your The Nature of True Virtue, *you argue that "the essence of true virtue" consists of a genuine love of being in general, which first and foremost must be rooted in a love for God.*[140]

JE: Yes, this is the case. "True virtue most essentially consists in benevolence for Being in general." But this must be understood in light of the fact "that true virtue must chiefly consist in love to God; the Being of beings, infinitely the greatest and best of beings." "The first Being, the eternal and infinite Being [God], is in effect, Being in general." A "truly virtuous mind, being as it were under the sovereign dominion of love to God, does above all things seek the glory of

God, and makes this his supreme, governing, and ultimate end." And "nothing is of the nature true virtue, in which God is not the first and the last."[141]

Is it correct to say, then that true virtue is really a love for God?

JE: Yes. "It may be asserted in general that nothing is of the nature of true virtue, in which God is not the first and the last. All that virtue which is saving, and distinguishing of true Christians from others, is summed up in Christian or divine love."[142]

This means that all true love must first and foremost be rooted in a love for God.

JE: Yes. "If a man has any true love to God, he must have a spirit to love God above all, because, without seeing something of the divine glory, there can be no true love to God; but if a man sees anything of divine glory, he will see that He is more glorious than any other; for whereinsoever God is divine, therein He is above all others. If men are sensible only of some excellency in God that is common with Him to others, they are not sensible of anything of His divine glory. But so far as any man is sensible of excellency in God above others, so far must he love Him above all others."[143]

Does this mean that a genuine love for God must be a love, not primarily for what one receives from God, but for God Himself?

JE: This is correct. "We are obliged not only to love Him with a love of gratitude for benefits received; but true love for God primarily consists in a supreme regard to Him for what He is in Himself."[144] "The first objective ground of gracious affections, is the transcendently excellent and amiable nature of divine things, as they are in themselves, and not any conceived relation they bear to self, or self-interest."[145]

Does this mean that there is not a proper type of self-love?

JE: No, "a Christian spirit is not contrary to all self-love."[146] That is, there is a proper self-love, because a biblically based self-love will see God as the highest good for the self, and will rejoice in and embrace God as the greatest good.[147] "Thus self-love is not excluded from a gracious gratitude. The saints do love God for His kindness to them.... But something else is included, for another love has already paved the way and laid the foundation for these grateful affections."[148] Therefore, "self-love duly regulated is a thing of great use in [Christian] religion."[149]

Justification

Justification immediately follows conversion, and according to the Shorter Catechism *(Q. 33), "justification is an act of God's free grace, wherein He pardons all our sins, and accepts us as righteous in His sight, only for the righteousness of Christ imputed to us, and received by faith alone." How do you define justification?*

JE: "Justification is not only pardon of sin...but in an act or sentence approving of him as innocent and positively righteous, and so having a right to freedom from punishment, and to the reward of positive righteousness.... But the pardon we have in Christ is a freeing persons from the punishment of sin, as an act of justice, and because they are looked upon and accepted as having that which is equivalent to innocence, *viz.* satisfaction.... Justification consists of imputing righteousness. To pardon sin is to cease to be angry for sin. But imputing righteousness and ceasing to be angry for sin are two things; one is the foundation of the other. God ceases to be angry with the sinner for his sin because [Christ's] righteousness is imputed to him."[150]

The doctrine of justification by grace alone, through faith alone, in Christ alone, was the central doctrine of the Reformation. You are a staunch defender of this doctrine.

JE: I am, indeed. "We are justified only by faith in Christ, and not by any manner of goodness of our own."[151] "They therefore that hold that sincere obedience is the condition of being in Christ…they maintain what is contrary to the Scripture doctrine of justification by faith alone."[152]

When you teach that justification is by faith alone, you do not mean that one's faith is in any sense meritorious, do you?

JE: No, neither faith nor repentance justify "as a work, for the nature of the one [repentance] is to renounce works, and the nature of the other [faith] is to depend on the work of another [Christ]."[153] "God does not give those that believe a union with or an interest in the Savior as a reward for faith, but only because faith is the soul's active uniting with Christ." "God looks on it fit by a natural fitness, that he whose heart sincerely unites itself to Christ as his Savior should be looked upon as united to that Savior, and so having an interest in Him."[154] Ultimately, of course, "if it is inquired what we must be saved for or on account of the answer is it must be for works, but not our works; nor for any works that we have done or can do but works that Christ has done for us."[155]

What about the Arminian view of saving faith, which tends to make faith a good work?

JE: This view is "fatal…. [It is] another gospel." The Arminians "entirely disclaim the popish doctrine of merit, and are free to speak of our utter unworthiness, and the great imperfection of all our services. But after all, it is our virtue, imperfect as it is, that recommends men to God…whether they will allow merit or no, yet they hold, that we are accepted by our merit, in the same sense, though not in the same degree, as under the first covenant [of works]."[156] "By them [the Arminians], salvation, is so far from God that it is God that gives opportunity to obtain salvation, it is God that gives the offer and makes the promises; but the obtaining the thing promised is of men."[157] "Arminianism…eats out the heart of [Christian] religion."[158]

I know that you also denounce the Arminian concept of conditions, wherein such conditions are to some degree meritorious ("the Arminian scheme of justification by our own virtue").[159]

JE: I do reject this view. "Talking thus, whether it be truly or falsely, is doubtless the foundation of Arminianism and neonomianism, and tends very much to make men value themselves for their own righteousness."[160]

Is this worse than Deism?

JE: No, Deism is worse. "The deists wholly cast off the Christian religion, and are professed infidels. They are not like the heretics, Arians and Socinians, and others, that own the Scriptures to be the Word of God, and hold the Christian religion to be the true religion, but only deny these and these fundamental doctrines of the Christian religion; they deny the whole Christian religion. Indeed, they own the being of God but deny the whole Scripture; they deny that any of it is the Word of God. They deny any revealed religion, or any Word of God at all, and say that God has given mankind no other light to walk by but his own reason."[161]

Roman Catholicism teaches the doctrine of congruent merit, i.e., that in some way the good works of man are meritorious.

JE: "Although, on account of faith in the believer, it is in the sight of God fit and congruous that he who believes should be looked upon both as in Christ and also as having an interest in His merits…yet it appears that this is very different from a merit of congruity, or indeed any moral congruity at all."[162]

You also teach, as have a number of Reformed theologians, including John Calvin and the Westminster divines, that faith and other graces (such as obedience and perseverance) are "conditions" of salvation, even though they are non-meritorious "conditions," because they all come as a gift of God.

JE: Yes, I do. "In one sense of the word Christ alone performs the condition of our salvation.... And in another sense of the word there are other graces besides faith that are the condition of justification." But "faith is that in them which God has respect to upon the account of which God judges it meet that they should by looked upon as Christ's righteousness belonging to them. God sees it meet that some men rather than others should have Christ's righteousness imputed to them."[163] We must remember that "faith itself is a gift of God, and that the saints' perseverance in a way of holiness unto glory, is also the fruit of electing love."[164] And perseverance is so "contained in the first act of faith," that it cannot possibly fail.[165] "The faith by which we are justified is [a] persevering faith."[166] We may correctly say that love and obedience are conditions of salvation because of "their necessary and immutable connection with [saving] faith, as immediately flowing from the nature of it."[167]

You are saying that as necessary as these graces are in order to salvation, they are gifts of God and non-meritorious and non-justifying; they are not in any sense instrumental in justification.

JE: Yes; "that which makes our obedience the matter of our justification...[is] contrary to the gospel doctrine of justification."[168]

In the Westminster Confession of Faith *(16:2), we read that "good works, done in obedience to God's commandments, are the fruits and evidences of a true and lively faith." Do you agree with this statement?*

JE: Yes, "good works [are the] proper evidences of godliness."[169] "Evangelical obedience...is an expression of [saving] faith."[170] The "universal obedience" to which God calls us, "is the proper evidence of our acceptable state" with God.[171]

You often speak of "universal obedience," or "universal holiness." What do you mean by this?

JE: By "universal holiness" I mean that the holiness of the

believer should "extend itself to all God's commands, and all employment and persons, all conditions, and all time."[172]

Where in the Scriptures do we see the nature of godliness most clearly set forth?

JE: "I know of no part of Holy Scripture, where the nature and evidences of true and sincere godliness, are so much of set purpose, and so fully and largely insisted on and delineated as in the 119th Psalm; the psalmist declares his design in the first verses of the Psalm, and he keeps his eye on this design all along, and pursues it to the end: but in the Psalm the excellency of holiness is represented as the immediate object of a spiritual taste, relish, appetite and delight, God's law, that grand expression and emanation of the holiness of God's nature, and prescription of holiness to the creature, is all along represented as the food and entertainment, and as the great object of love, the appetite, the complacence and rejoicing of the gracious nature, which prizes God's commandments above gold, yea, the finest gold, and to which they are sweeter than the honey, and honeycomb; and that upon account of their holiness."[173]

The Confession *(16:7) also states that for a good work to be a good work it must be done for the glory of God.*

JE: This is also correct; "no actions are good but what have the honor of God as their chief end proposed."[174]

Augustine once said that "when God rewards our merits, He crowns His own gifts." Is this the case? Does God reward these good works?

JE: Yes, He does. "He has a propensity to reward holiness, but He gives it on purpose that He may reward it."[175] Remember that "good works, though they are done in sincerity and from true love to God, and though they are real exercises of true grace, don't in themselves deserve anything from God. When the saints do duties from love to God, and with a gracious respect to Him, they do no more than is commanded of them.... Though God is under no natural obligation to reward your obedience, however fervent and perfect, yet He is pleased to oblige Himself to reward forever in heaven every good work that is performed in sincerity, every act that is done from a gracious respect unto Him."[176] "But when God rewards the good works of believers, it is in testimony of His respect to the loveliness of their good works in Christ: for their good works are not lovely to God in themselves, but they are lovely to Him in Christ and beholding them not separately and by themselves, but as in Christ."[177]

I know that you are aware that the Roman Catholic Church teaches that some men are able to do works of supererogation, i.e., that they are able to do works over and above what God requires. What is your response?

JE: "There are none of fallen men but, after all that they have done, they have done but a little part of that which is mere duty. They are so far from any work of supererogation or doing anything over and above what God is indebted for that it is but a small part of that which is their absolute duty to perform."[178]

Adoption

Adoption, like justification, is considered to be a judicial act of God, and that in adoption God brings the justified sinner into a filial relationship with Himself.

JE: This is precisely so. "Christians are the children of God, as partaking with Christ, the only-begotten Son, in His sonship."[179]

You deny then the errant teaching that says that all men are the children of God.

JE: I do. As I just commented, "Christians are the children of God."

Certainly you do not deny, though, that God is good even to the nonbeliever, do you?

JE: No; "God is kind to the unthankful and to the evil, and this appears in His great kindness to mankind who are the subjects of abundance of the kindness and goodness of God and yet are very evil and unthankful."[180]

Sanctification

Sanctification is the central and most emphasized theme of your sermons. Even though salvation is by faith alone, that faith is not alone. If it is genuine faith, it is always accompanied by good works in the process of sanctification. Sanctification is a necessary corollary to justification.

JE: This is correct.

In the Westminster Larger Catechism *(Q. 77), the divines stated that "although sanctification be inseparably joined with justification, yet they differ, in that God in justification imputes the righteousness of Christ; in sanctification His Spirit infuses grace, and enables to the exercise thereof." How do you view this?*

JE: This is proper teaching. "There is a two-fold righteousness which the saints have: an imputed righteousness, and it is this only that avails anything to justification; and an inherent righteousness, that is, that holiness and grace which is in the hearts and lives of the saints. This is Christ's righteousness as well as imputed righteousness: imputed righteousness is Christ's righteousness accepted for them, inherent holiness is Christ's communicated to them.... Now God takes delight in the saints for both of these: both for Christ's righteousness imputed and for Christ's holiness communicated, though it is the former only that avails anything for justification."[181]

In the Westminster Confession of Faith *(11:2), we read: "Faith, thus receiving and resting on Christ and His righteousness, is the alone instrument of justification; yet it is not alone in the person justified, but is ever accompanied with all other saving graces, and is no dead faith, but works by love." Do you agree with the second part of this statement, i.e., that saving faith is always accompanied by good works?*

JE: Yes: "There is no room left for anyone to say that they have faith which justifies and that they need take no care about works and so to give themselves the liberty in sinning because they are not under the law but under grace; for though it is only faith that justifies yet there is no faith that justifies but a working faith; so that it is impossible for any person should be saved without works as if they were justified upon the account of their works. It is impossible that men should be saved without an evangelical, universal, and sincere obedience under the second covenant [of grace] as it was that they should be saved without a perfect obedience under the first covenant [of works]."[182] Thus, "Men are not saved on account of any work of theirs, and yet they are not saved without works."[183] "A true trust in Christ is never infused without other graces with it."[184]

I would also add that the good works of the justified saint must be "universal" if a true conversion is involved, because a genuine conversion affects every area of the believer's life. And although all of his good works are tainted with sin, they are "universal" in scope; there is a "beautiful symmetry and proportion" of "holy affections," wherein the practice of godliness is the whole "business" of one's life. All is consciously done for the glory of God.[185] I believe "that converts are new men, new creatures, that they [are] renewed not only within, but without, that old things are passed away, and all things become new, that whereas they before were the servants of sin, and yielded their members servants of iniquity to iniquity, now they yield them servants of righteousness unto holiness."[186] "The spirit that godly men are of is a spirit to be perfectly holy."[187] True godliness, then, "consists not in a heart to purpose to do the will of God, but in an heart to do it."[188]

But the process of sanctification involves a constant warfare, does it not?

JE: There is a "mutual opposition and strife" that exists "between grace and corruption in the hearts of the saints during their continuance in this world."[189] The struggle in the life of the believer is likened to "Rebecca, in having Esau and Jacob struggle together in her womb."[190] That is, "conversion does not entirely root out the natural temper" of the saint, but now the "evil dispositions...shall no longer constitute the person's character."[191]

Are you here making a distinction between one's initial "conversion" and later "conversions?" That is, there is only one "conversion" in the life of any Christian, which, as noted above, occurs when he responds in faith and repentance to the call of the gospel. At the same time, there must also be numerous "conversions" in a believer's life, which occur when he progressively confesses and forsakes sin in his life.

JE: This is precisely so. "Those that have true grace in their hearts [Christians] may yet stand in great need of being converted."[192] One of the "signs of godliness" is that of "humility, a broken and contrite heart, a being poor in spirit, sensibleness of our own vileness and unworthiness, self-abasement, disclaiming all worthiness and glory, mourning for sin."[193]

One of the more controversial passages in the Bible on this subject is Romans 7:14-25. Is Paul speaking here as a converted man or an unconverted man?

JE: "The apostle here speaks in the name of a true saint, and not in the name of a wicked man."[194]

It is true, then, that the believer does indeed struggle with indwelling sin?

JE: Yes, he does. "There is an abundance of corruption in the hearts of [God's people]." Sadly, there are times when they "walk in evil ways" and manifest "such kinds of sin and corruption that they never imagined were in the hearts of the godly." They, like non-believers sometimes "slumber and sleep." But in the end "their religion cannot be said to fail." God will preserve them.[195]

Martin Luther once said that the entire Christian life is one of repentance. What do you think about this statement?

JE: Luther was correct; "we should constantly be confessing and forsaking our sins before God."[196] "God's people ought to be much in reflecting on their sins and humbling themselves for them after they have evidences of God's having forgiven them."[197]

When you speak of "signs of godliness" what exactly are you referring to?

JE: There are "two sorts of signs of godliness": one is internal and the other external. The internal signs are "such as seeing and knowing God and spiritually understanding divine things; believing the reality of divine things; loving God, fearing God, trusting in God; repentance; believing in Christ; choosing and resting in God and Christ," etc. The external signs are "bringing forth fruit, doing good works, keeping God's and Christ's commandments universally and perseveringly, mortifying our lusts, denying ourselves... being of a Christian temper and behavior towards ourselves and our fellow creatures." Both the internal and the external signs "are given in Scripture as signs by which we are to try our sincerity by, and by which we are to try whether we indeed have those things wherein godliness more radically consists."[198]

Could you please expand on this a bit more?

JE: Certainly. "The internal acts and principals of the worship of God, or the worship of the heart, in the love and fear of God, trust in God, and resignation to God, etc., are the most essential and important of all duties of religion whatsoever; for therein consists the essence of all religion. But of this inward religion, there are two sorts of external manifestations or expressions. The one sort are outward acts of worship, such as meeting in religious assemblies, attending sacraments and other outward institutions, and honoring God with gestures, such as bowing, or kneeling before Him, or with words, in speaking honorably of Him in prayer, praise, or religious conference. And the other sort are the expressions of our love to God by obeying His moral commands of self-denial, righteousness, meekness, and Christian love, in our behavior among men. And the latter are of vastly the greatest importance in the Christian life. God makes little account of the former in comparison of them.... Hypocrites and self-righteous persons do much more commonly abound in the former kind of duties than the latter."[199]

Is this why you stress that men must continue to "seek" subsequent to their conversion? Now, however, they are not seeking for conversion, but for their continual growth in the Lord.

JE: Yes, it is. "The apostle [Paul] did not only thus earnestly seek salvation before his conversion and hope, but afterwards [as well]. What he says in the third [chapter] of Philippians of his suffering the loss of all things, that he might be found in Christ, and its being the one thing that he did to seek salvation; and also what he says of his so running as not uncertainly, but as resolving to win the prize of salvation, and keeping under his body that he might not be a castaway; was long after his conversion and after he had received his hope of his own good estate. If being already converted excuses a man from seeking salvation any more, or makes it reasonable that he should leave off his earnest care and labor for it, certainly the apostle might have been excused, when he had not only already attained true grace, but such eminent degrees of it. To see one of the most eminent saints that ever lived, if not the most eminent of all, so exceedingly engaged in seeking his own salvation—it ought for ever to put to shame those that are a thousand degrees below him, and are but mere infants to him, if they have any grace at all; that yet excuse themselves from using any violence after the kingdom of heaven now, because they have attained already, easing themselves of the burden of going on earnestly to seek salvation with this, that they have got through the work, they have got a hope. The apostle, as eminent as he was, did not say within himself, 'I am converted, and so am sure of salvation. Christ has promised it to me; what need I care any further about obtaining salvation? Yea, I am not only converted, but I have obtained great degrees of grace.' The apostle knew that though he was converted, yet there remained a great work that he must do, in order to his [final] salvation. There was a narrow way to eternal glory, that he must pass through and never could come to the crown of glory any other way. He knew that it was absolutely necessary for him earnestly to seek salvation still; he knew that there was no going to heaven in a lazy way."[200]

Would you say that holiness is both the desire and the goal of the saint?

JE: I would, indeed. The saint delights in holiness out of a love for God, who is the ultimate producer of holiness: "Holiness is…the highest beauty and amiableness…. It makes the soul a little sweet and delightful image of the blessed *Jehovah*…. What a sweet calmness, what calm ecstasies, does it bring to the soul…. It makes the soul like…a garden planted by God…where the sun is Jesus Christ, the blessed beams and calm breeze, the Holy Spirit."[201] For the saint, there is an "inward burning desire…a holy breathing and panting after the Spirit of God, to increase holiness, [which is] as natural to a holy nature as breathing is to a living body."[202]

The Bible frequently speaks of the "fear of God," but there is a fear of God that the non-believer has also, is there not?

JE: Yes. "Herein is the difference between a godly fear, or the fear of a godly man, and the fear of a sinner: the one [the sinner] fears the effects of God's displeasure, the other [the godly man] fears His displeasure itself."[203]

You believe that the process of sanctification necessarily involves the usage of the "means of grace" – primarily Scripture, the sacraments, and prayer.[204] This being so, it is not possible for a Christian to grow spiritually without a knowledge of the Word of God.

JE: Correct. Therefore, "every Christian should make a business of endeavoring to grow in knowledge of divinity.... There is no other way by which any means of grace whatsoever can be of any benefit, but by knowledge.... Christians ought not to content themselves with such degrees of knowledge in divinity as they have already obtained. It should not satisfy them that they know as much as is absolutely necessary to salvation, but should seek to make progress.... However diligently we apply ourselves, there is room enough to increase our knowledge of divinity, without coming to an end." Christians, then, must grow in knowledge. "If persons have ever tasted the sweetness of the Word and grace of Christ they will be longing for more and more of it."[205] And all knowledge is conveyed by the Spirit of God to the elect of God, by means of the Word and the sacraments as they are explained and understood in accordance with the Word.[206] "The Scripture speaks of the Word of God as the principal means of carrying on God's work; for the Word of God is the principal means nevertheless, as that is the means by which other means operate, and are made effectual: the sacraments have no effect but by the Word...for all that is visible to the eye is unintelligible and vain, without the Word of God to instruct and guide the mind."[207] Also, "God's Spirit always attends His ordinances."[208] And "conversion is wrought by the Word and ordinances."[209]

In this process of sanctification, Christ rules over His people, but at the same time He does not force them to be holy.

JE: Not at all. He "does not force them, but sweetly inclines their wills to the most excellent things and to their own happiness. He overcomes them by His love; He governs them by infusing love into them, and so inclining them to obedience. His dominion over His people is by mutual love and esteem."[210]

We have already talked at some length about prayer, but you believe as well that prayer is essential to the process of sanctification. In His Word, God speaks to His people; in prayer, they speak to Him. Herein there is communion between God and His elect.

JE: Indeed, prayer is essential. As you have said, biblical Christianity maintains that "God ought to be worshipped by prayer, confession, praise, and thanksgiving, and those duties in which we speak to God." And in the Bible, God "speaks to us."[211] "Conversation between God and mankind in this world is maintained by God's Word on His part, and prayer on ours. By the former He speaks to us and expresses His mind to us; by the latter we speak to Him and express our minds to Him."[212] For God's people, there is "the great duty of secret prayer."[213] "The true spirit of prayer is no other than God's own Spirit dwelling in the hearts of the saints. And as this Spirit comes from God, so does it naturally tend to God in holy breathings [and] pantings.... True prayer is nothing else but faith expressed.... True prayer is the faith and reliance of the soul breathed forth in words."[214]

Even though there will be no more sin to wage war against in the final state, will the process of sanctification (increasing in holiness) continue forever?

JE: Yes. "There are many reasons to think that what God has in view, in an increasing communication of Himself through eternity, is an increasing knowledge of God, love to Him, and joy in Him. And it is to be considered that the more those divine communications increase in the creature, the more it becomes one with God; for so much the more it is united to God in love, the heart is drawn nearer and nearer to God, and union with Him becomes more firm and close, and at the same time the creature becomes more and more conformed to God. The image is more and more perfect, and so the good that is in the creature comes for ever nearer and nearer to an identity to that which is in God. In the view therefore of God, who has a comprehensive prospect of the increasing union and conformity through eternity, it must be an infinitely strict and perfect nearness, conformity, and oneness. For it will for ever come nearer and nearer to that strictness and perfection of union which there is between the Father and the Son."[215]

Perseverance

The doctrine of the perseverance of the saints is not one and the same thing with assurance of salvation. Whereas perseverance teaches that no Christian will finally fall away from the state of salvation to which God has brought him, assurance has to do with the individual Christian's confidence of his own state. A justified man may doubt his salvation, but this does not deny the doctrine of perseverance.

JE: This is an accurate statement.

How is it that perseverance is a condition of salvation?

JE: "Perseverance in holiness is absolutely necessary to salvation," because a genuine saving faith is a persevering faith.[216] "It is necessary for those that have religious affections and seem to have a love to Christ that they should endure to the end in order to their being saved."[217] Perseverance "is the only way to heaven, [it is] the narrow way that leads to life."[218] "You must never expect to go to heaven in any other than a strait and narrow way.... If you would go to heaven, you must be content to go there in the way of self-denial and sufferings; you must be willing to take up the cross daily and follow Christ."[219]

Is this the error of the hypocrites?

JE: Yes, it is. "Hypocrites never counted the cost of perseverance in seeking God, and of following Him to the end of life."[220]

And yet, it is not possible that a genuine Christian will not persevere; is this not correct?

JE: That is correct. The reason being that "God, in the act of justification, which is passed on a sinner's first believing, has respect to perseverance, as being virtually contained in that first act of faith."[221] God's "promise of acceptance is made only to a persevering sort of faith."[222] The believer is in union with Jesus Christ, and he cannot ever permanently fall away from the faith.[223] A true Christian may indeed fall into sin, but God will keep him from continuing in it.[224] "That the saints shall surely persevere, will necessarily follow this," that "the righteousness by which they have justification unto life" has "already been performed for them [by Christ] and imputed to them" in Christ.[225]

So then, saints are unable to persevere in their own strength.

JE: Again, this is correct. "There is not only a gate that must be entered, but there is a narrow way that must be traveled before we can arrive at heavenly blessedness. And that is a way of universal and persevering holiness. But men… cannot persevere in a way of holiness of themselves. But there is sufficient provision made for this also in the way of salvation by Jesus Christ. The matter of the saint's perseverance is sufficiently secured by the purchase that Christ has made."[226]

Assurance

Can one be assured of his salvation?

JE: Yes, there is "an absolute sort of certainty" that one can have.[227] There are certain "marks of a work of the true Spirit" that reveal a genuine work of conversion.[228] Herein "true grace [is] distinguished from the experience of devils."[229]

Does this assurance come from an inner witness, or in some other way?

JE: Both. There is, to be sure, an inner witness of assurance given to the elect by the Holy Spirit. Nevertheless, "assurance is not to be obtained as much by self-examination as it is by action."[230] "That which distinguishes good men from bad is not that they hear good, profess good, or intend good, but that they do good. They are workers of good."[231]

What does Paul refer to in Romans 8:16, where he says that "the Spirit Himself bears witness with our spirit that we are children of God?"

JE: "Sometimes the strong and lively exercises of love to God do give a kind of immediate and intuitive evidence of the soul's relation to God.... The Spirit of God gives those motions and exercises of a childlike love to God that naturally inclines the heart to look on God as his Father and behave towards Him as such."[232]

Are there any sure evidences or marks of the work of the Holy Spirit, wherein a person can be assured that he is a Christian?

JE: Yes, there are. From a study of 1 John 4 we learn that there are several "sure, distinguishing evidences and marks of a work of the Spirit of God." First, "the operation [of the Holy Spirit] exalts Jesus.... The Spirit begets in people higher and more honorable thoughts of Christ than they used to have and to incline their affections more to Him." Second, "the Spirit attacks Satan's interests." Third, "the Spirit exalts the Holy Scriptures...[and] lifts up sound doctrine." And fourth, "the Spirit promotes love to God and man." "When a spirit operates after this manner among people, there is the highest kind of evidence of the influence of a true and divine Spirit."[233]

And the surest sign of all?

JE: Christian practice. "Herein chiefly appears the power of true godliness, *viz.* in its being effectual in practice." This is the "chief of all the marks of grace, the sign of signs, and evidence of evidences, that which seals and crowns all other signs."[234] "So that keeping Christ's commands is the highest evidence of a good estate, and yet the witness of the Spirit of adoption or love is the highest evidence: for they are both the same."[235]

It is not just talking about the Christian faith, then, it is practicing it.

JE: Precisely so. "Christ nowhere says, You shall know the tree by its leaves or flowers, or you shall know men by their talk, or you shall know them by the good story they tell of their experiences, or you shall know them by the manner and air of their speaking, and emphasis and pathos of expression, or by their speaking feelingly, or by making a very great show by abundance of talk."[236]

And where or when is this practice most noticeable?

JE: During times of trial. "The experience Christians have by their enduring trials [of their faith] give the highest ground of hope."[237] The "external religion of false Christians [is likely] to fail in times of trial." But true Christians "cannot be said to fail as the religion of hypocrites is wont to do at such times, because their declining is not of the nature as to carry in them a practical casting off God and [Christian] religion."[238]

Is assurance necessary for salvation?

JE: No, it is not. "That a believing that I am in a good estate is no part or ingredient in the essence of saving faith, is evident by this, that the essence of saving faith must complete in me before it can be true that I am in a good estate. If I haven't as yet acted faith, yea, if there be anything wanting in me to make up the essence of saving faith, then I am not as yet in a state of salvation, and therefore can have no ground to believe that I am so."[239] "All those that are converted, are not sure of it; and those who are sure of it, do not know that they shall always be so."[240]

Ultimately we cannot see the hearts of men. Surely the church has the responsibility to make judgments about the spiritual state of others; yet, some theologians seem to be quick to make precipitous judgments against others, condemning them rather quickly.

JE: "The longer I live, the less I wonder that God keeps it as His right to try the hearts of the children of men. Also I wonder less that God directs that this business should be let alone to the harvest. I adore the wisdom of God! In His goodness to me and my fellow creatures, He has not committed this great business into our hands…. He has committed it into the hands of One infinitely fitter for it and has made it His own right."[241] "I once did not imagine that the heart of man had been so unsearchable as I find it is…. I find more things in wicked men that may counterfeit, and make a fair show of piety, and more ways that the remaining corruption of the godly may make them appear like carnal men, formalists, and dead hypocrites, than once I knew it."[242]

What would be the best scriptural example of this, i.e., that ministers should not be too quick to judge the state of one's soul?

JE: Perhaps the best example is that of Jesus Christ and Judas Iscariot. He "was one of the twelve apostles, and had long been constantly united to, and intimately conversant with, a company of truly experienced disciples, without being discovered or suspected, till he discovered himself by his scandalous practice. He had been treated by Jesus Himself, in all external things, as if he had truly been a disciple, even investing him with the character of apostle, sending him forth to preach the gospel, and enduing him with miraculous gifts of the Spirit. For though Christ knew him, yet He did not then clothe Himself with the character of omniscient Judge, and searcher of hearts, but acted the part of a minister of the visible church…and therefore rejected him not, till he had discovered himself by his scandalous practice; thereby giving an example to guides and rulers of the visible church, not to take it upon them to act the part of searcher of hearts, but to be influenced in their administrations by what is visible and open."[243]

The Puritans were very aware of the problem of self-deception. So isn't there a danger involved with this doctrine of assurance?

JE: Indeed, there is. "And nothing is more common than for men to be mistaken concerning their own state. Many that are abominable to God, and the children of His wrath, think highly of themselves, as His precious saints and dear children."[244] "It is a very common thing for men…to imagine that they are converted when they are not converted."[245]

What is the best piece of advice you could give to young converts regarding their continuing in the Christian faith, especially those who are in need of assurance?

JE: We must remember that "we have an advocate with the Father, Jesus Christ the righteous, the preciousness of whose blood, and the merit of whose righteousness, and the greatness of whose love and faithfulness does infinitely overtop the highest mountains of our sins…. One new discovery of the glory of Christ's face, and the fountain of His sweet grace and love will do more towards scattering clouds of darkness and doubting in one minute, than examining old experiences by the best mark that can be given, a whole year…. [Therefore] in all your course, walk with God and follow Christ as a little, poor, helpless child, taking hold of Christ's hand, keeping your eye on the mark of the wounds on His hands and side, whence came the blood that cleanses you from sin and hiding your nakedness under the skirt of the white shining robe of His righteousness."[246]

Glorification

This is the final stage of the ordo salutis, *and we will discuss it later.*

JE: Very well.

---

[1] Edwards, *Works* (Yale), 21:294.
[2] Edwards, *Sermon* on 1 Corinthians 1:29-31.
[3] Edwards, *Works*, II:557.
[4] Edwards, *Works* (Yale), 14:435.
[5] Edwards, *Works* (Yale), 9:116.
[6] Edwards, *Miscellany* 814.
[7] Edwards, *Sermon* on Matthew 10:17.
[8] Edwards, *Works* (Yale), 16:481.
[9] Edwards, *Works* (Yale), 11:124.
[10] Edwards, *Sermon* on 2 Peter 2:14.
[11] Edwards, *Sermon* on Hebrews 13:8.
[12] Edwards, *Miscellany* 436.
[13] Edwards, *Miscellany* 290.
[14] Edwards, *Works* (Yale), 3:389-409.
[15] Edwards, *Sermon* on Romans 7:14.
[16] Edwards, *Works* (Yale), 5:345.
[17] Edwards, *Sermon* on Luke 13:5.
[18] Edwards, *Sermon* on Romans 7:14.
[19] Edwards, *Miscellany* 386.
[20] Edwards, *Works* (Yale), 4:394.
[21] Edwards, *Works* (Yale), 3:251.
[22] Edwards, *Miscellany* 797.
[23] Edwards, *Works*, I:152-153.
[24] Edwards, *Miscellany* 965.
[25] Edwards, *Sermon* on Ezekiel 15:2-4.
[26] Edwards, *Standing in Grace*, edited by Don Kistler, 30.
[27] Edwards, *Works* (Yale), 16:91ff.
[28] Edwards, *Miscellany* 1010.
[29] Edwards, *Miscellany* 1032.
[30] Edwards, *Miscellany* 380.
[31] Edwards, *Miscellany* 706.
[32] Edwards, *Miscellany* 703.
[33] Edwards, *Works* (Yale), 9:117-119; *Works*, II:599; *Miscellany* 30.
[34] Edwards, *Miscellany* 399.
[35] Edwards, *Sermon* on Romans 4:5.
[36] Edwards, *Miscellany* 1353.
[37] Edwards, *Works* (Yale), 11:228.
[38] Edwards, *Works* (Yale), 9:290.

[39] Edwards, *Works* (Yale), 11:204.
[40] Edwards, *Miscellany* 27b.
[41] Edwards, *Works* (Yale), 9:443.
[42] Edwards, *Sermon* on Matthew 22:14.
[43] Edwards, *Works* (Yale), 13:13.
[44] Edwards, *Works* (Yale), 9:398.
[45] Edwards, *Miscellanies* 663, 840, 884.
[46] Edwards, *Works* (Yale), 11:204.
[47] Edwards, *Works* (Yale), 20:110n.
[48] Edwards, *Sermon* on Isaiah 6:5.
[49] Cited in *Our Great and Glorious God*, 92.
[50] Cited in McDermott, *Jonathan Edwards Confronts the Gods*, 159.
[51] Edwards, *Works* (Yale), 21:405.
[52] Edwards, *Miscellany* 959.
[53] Edwards, *Works* (Yale), 15:370-371.
[54] Edwards, *Miscellany* 840.
[55] Edwards, *Sermon* on Romans 9:18.
[56] Gerstner, *Jonathan Edwards: Evangelist*, 18-23.
[57] Edwards, *Sermon* on Romans 8:29.
[58] Edwards, *Sermon* on Hosea 13:9.
[59] Edwards, *Sermon* on Isaiah 53:10; *Sermon* on Romans 8:29; *Sermon* on John 16:8.
[60] Edwards, *Sermon* on Ephesians 3:10.
[61] Edwards, *Sermon* on Zechariah 4:7.
[62] Edwards, *Sermon* on John 16:8.
[63] Edwards, *Standing in Grace*, 56, 62.
[64] Edwards, *Standing in Grace*, 1-2.
[65] Edwards, *Miscellany* 427.
[66] Edwards, *Sermon* on Romans 4:5.
[67] Edwards, *Miscellany* 1091.
[68] Edwards, *Works* (Yale), 21:444.
[69] Edwards, *Works* (Yale), 3:386.
[70] Cited in Gerstner, *The Rational Biblical Theology of Jonathan Edwards*, III:222-223.
[71] Edwards, *Sermon* on Habakkuk 2:4.
[72] Edwards, *Works* (Yale), 2:203.
[73] Edwards, *Miscellanies* 315, 393.
[74] Edwards, *Works* (Yale), 9:124.
[75] Edwards, *Sermon* on Revelation 3:20.
[76] Edwards, *Sermon* on Matthew 13:23; *Sermon* on Matthew 16:17; *Miscellany* 1299.
[77] Edwards, *Sermon* on Matthew 22:14.
[78] Edwards, *Sermon* on Amos 8:11; *Sermon* on Romans 1:24.
[79] Edwards, *Miscellany* 814.

[80] Edwards, *Works* (Yale), 14:365.
[81] Edwards, *Works* (Yale), 4:28.
[82] Edwards, *Sermon* on Genesis 6:22.
[83] Edwards, *Sermon* on Ecclesiastes 4:5.
[84] Edwards, *Sermon* on Ecclesiastes 9:10.
[85] Edwards, *Sermon* on Proverbs 28:13.
[86] Edwards, *Sermon* on Psalm 25:11.
[87] Edwards, *Miscellany* 522.
[88] Edwards, *Miscellany* 538.
[89] Edwards, *Sermon* on 2 Kings 7:3-4.
[90] Edwards, *Works* (Yale), 2:418.
[91] Cited in Anri Morimoto, *Jonathan Edwards and the Catholic Vision of Salvation*, 27.
[92] Cited in Stephen J. Nichols, *A Guided Tour of His Life and Thought*, 97.
[93] Edwards, *Works* (Yale), 21:483n.
[94] Edwards, *Works* (Yale), 15:285.
[95] Edwards, *Sermon* on John 16:8.
[96] Edwards, *Sermon* on John 16:8.
[97] Edwards, *Sermon* on Matthew 16:17.
[98] Edwards, *Miscellany* 397.
[99] Edwards, *Sermon* on John 3:3.
[100] Edwards, *Miscellany* 15.
[101] Edwards, *Works*, II:543.
[102] Edwards, *Sermon* on John 3:7; see also *Miscellany* 617.
[103] Edwards, *Sermon* on 2 Corinthians 3:18.
[104] Edwards, *Sermon* on Song of Songs 5:1.
[105] Edwards, "Treatise on Grace," cited in Grosart, *Selections From the Unpublished Writings of Jonathan Edwards*, 37.
[106] Edwards, *Miscellany* 15.
[107] Edwards, *Sermon* on John 3:10-11.
[108] Edwards, *Sermon* on 1 Corinthians 6:11.
[109] Edwards, *Sermon* on 2 Peter 1:16.
[110] Edwards, *Miscellany* 397.
[111] Edwards, *Sermon* on Matthew 16:17.
[112] Edwards, *Sermon* on 2 Corinthians 3:18.
[113] Edwards, *Sermon* on 2 Corinthians 3:18.
[114] Edwards, *Works* (Yale), 8:331.
[115] Edwards, *Miscellany* 943.
[116] Edwards, *Miscellany* 504.
[117] Edwards, *Works*, I:213.
[118] Cited in Gerald R. McDermott, *Seeing God: Jonathan Edwards and Spiritual Discernment*, 71.
[119] Edwards, editor, *The Life and Diary of David Brainerd*, 78.
[120] Edwards, *Works* (Yale), 21:434.

[121] Edwards, *Works*, II:580.
[122] Edwards, *Works* (Yale), 21:356.
[123] Edwards, *Sermon* on Matthew 13:5.
[124] Edwards, *Sermon* on 1 John 1:5.
[125] Cited in *Devotions From the Pen of Jonathan Edwards*, 93, 97.
[126] Edwards, *Sermon* on 1 Corinthians 1:29-31.
[127] Edwards, *Miscellany* 317.
[128] The normal way of referring to this trio is *notitia* (knowledge), *assensus* (assent), and *fiducia* (trust).
[129] Edwards, *Works*, II:580.
[130] Edwards, *Sermon* on Galatians 5:6.
[131] Edwards, *Works* (Yale), 15:242.
[132] Edwards, *Sermon* on Matthew 16:17.
[133] Edwards, *Miscellany* ee.
[134] Edwards, *Sermon* on John 3:3.
[135] Edwards, *Sermon* on Matthew 25:1-12.
[136] Edwards, *Sermon* on Ephesians 4:24.
[137] Edwards, *Sermon* on Psalm 73:25.
[138] Edwards, *Sermon* on Matthew 16:17.
[139] Edwards, *Sermon* on Galatians 3:13-14.
[140] Edwards, *Works* (Yale), 8:537-627.
[141] Edwards, *Works* (Yale), 8:540, 550, 461, 559-560.
[142] Edwards, *Works* (Yale), 8:560, 131.
[143] Edwards, *Miscellany* 567.
[144] Edwards, *Works* (Yale), 3:144.
[145] Edwards, *Works*, I:317.
[146] Edwards, *Works* (Yale), 8:254.
[147] Edwards, *Miscellany* 530.
[148] Edwards, *Religious Affections*, 94.
[149] Edwards, *Sermon* on Proverbs 19:8.
[150] Edwards, *Miscellany* 812.
[151] Edwards, *Sermon* on Romans 4:5.
[152] Edwards, *Miscellany* 647.
[153] Edwards, *Miscellany* 620.
[154] Edwards, *Sermon* on Romans 4:5.
[155] Edwards, *Sermon* on Genesis 6:22.
[156] Edwards, *Sermon* on Romans 4:5.
[157] Edwards, *Works* (Yale), 21:279.
[158] Edwards, *Sermon* on Jeremiah 2:5.
[159] Edwards, *Works* (Yale), 18:13.
[160] Edwards, *Miscellany* 2.
[161] Edwards, *Works* (Yale), 9:432.
[162] Edwards, *Sermon* on Romans 4:5.
[163] Edwards, *Sermon* on Romans 4:16.

[164] Edwards, *Sermon* on 1 Peter 2:9.
[165] Edwards, *Sermon* on Romans 4:5.
[166] Edwards, *Works* (Yale), 21:360.
[167] Edwards, *Miscellany* 412.
[168] Edwards, *Miscellany* 474.
[169] Edwards, *Miscellany* 790.
[170] Edwards, *Miscellany* 670.
[171] Edwards, *Sermon* on Romans 4:5.
[172] Edwards, *Sermon* on 1 Peter 1:15.
[173] Edwards, *Works* (Yale), 2:260.
[174] Edwards, *Miscellany* 270.
[175] Edwards, *Miscellany* 589.
[176] Edwards, *Sermon* on Luke 17:9.
[177] Edwards, *Miscellany* 627.
[178] Edwards, *Sermon* on Luke 17:9.
[179] Edwards, *Sermon* on Romans 2:10.
[180] Edwards, *Sermon* on Luke 6:35.
[181] Edwards, *Sermon* on Titus 3:5, in *Works* (Yale), 14:340ff.
[182] Edwards, *Sermon* on Galatians 5:6.
[183] Edwards, *Sermon* on Genesis 6:22.
[184] Edwards, *Sermon* on Micah 3:11.
[185] Edwards, *Religious Affections*, 157ff.; *Sermon* on Zechariah 7:5-6.
[186] Edwards, *Works* (Yale), 16:228.
[187] Edwards, *Sermon* on Psalm 119:3.
[188] Edwards, *Sermon* on Deuteronomy 5:27-29.
[189] Edwards, *Sermon* on Galatians 5:17.
[190] Edwards, *Miscellany* 673.
[191] Edwards, *Works* (Yale), 2:341-342.
[192] Edwards, *Sermon* on Luke 22:32.
[193] Edwards, *Works* (Yale), 18:169.
[194] Cited in Grosart, *Selections From the Writings of Jonathan Edwards*, 153.
[195] Edwards, *Sermon* on Matthew 25:1-12.
[196] Cited in John H. Gerstner, "The Theology of Jonathan Edwards," a tape series.
[197] Edwards, *Sermon* on Ezekiel 16:63.
[198] Edwards, *Works* (Yale), 21:494-495.
[199] Edwards, *Works* (Yale), 4:522-523.
[200] Edwards, *Sermon* on Philippians 3:17.
[201] Edwards, *Miscellany* a.
[202] Edwards, *Works* (Yale), 2:382-383.
[203] Edwards, *Miscellany* 277.
[204] Edwards, *Miscellany* 539.
[205] Edwards, *Sermon* on 1 Peter 2:2.
[206] Edwards, *Sermon* on Hebrews 5:12.

[207] Edwards, *Works* (Yale), 4:240.
[208] Edwards, *Works*, I:539.
[209] Edwards, *Sermon* on John 3:3.
[210] Edwards, *Works* (Yale), 14:427.
[211] Edwards, *Miscellany* 749.
[212] Edwards, *Miscellany* 1338.
[213] Edwards, *Sermon* on Psalm 65:2.
[214] Edwards, *Sermon* on Job 27:10.
[215] Edwards, *Works*, I:101.
[216] Edwards, *Sermon* on Hebrews 10:38-39.
[217] Edwards, *Sermon* on Matthew 24:12-13.
[218] Edwards, *Sermon* on Isaiah 35:8.
[219] Edwards, *Sermon* on Romans 2:10.
[220] Edwards, *Sermon* on Job 27:10.
[221] Edwards, *Sermon* on Romans 4:5.
[222] Edwards, *Works*, II:596.
[223] Edwards, *Sermon* on 1 Timothy 2:5.
[224] Edwards, *Sermon* on Revelation 17:14.
[225] Edwards, *Works*, II:597.
[226] Edwards, *Sermon* on Ephesians 3:10.
[227] Edwards, *Works* (Yale), 6:346.
[228] Edwards, *Sermon* on 1 John 4:1.
[229] Edwards, *Sermon* on James 2:19.
[230] Edwards, *Sermon* on 1 Corinthians 9:26.
[231] Edwards, *Sermon* on Romans 2:10.
[232] Edwards, *Miscellany* 686.
[233] Cited in Parrish and Sproul, *The Spirit of Revival*, 87-98.
[234] Edwards, *Works* (Yale), 2:393, 443.
[235] Edwards, *Miscellany* 790.
[236] Edwards, *Works* (Yale), 2:407.
[237] Edwards, *Sermon* on Matthew 7:15.
[238] Edwards, *Sermon* on Matthew 25:1-12.
[239] Edwards, *Works* (Yale), 16:330.
[240] Edwards, *Sermon* on Hebrews 9:13-14.
[241] Cited in Parrish and Sproul, *The Spirit of Revival*, 140-141.
[242] Edwards, *Works* (Yale), 4:285.
[243] Edwards, *Works*, II:265.
[244] Edwards, *Works*, I:cci.
[245] Edwards, *Sermon* on Matthew 15:26.
[246] Edwards, *Works* (Yale), 16:91ff.

CHAPTER 9
Edwards on the Church

What is the church of Jesus Christ?

JE: "The Christian church is the temple of God, and particular believers are the stones of which that temple is built.... And Christ is the foundation of this building, or the chief corner stone."[1] The church is the "spouse of the Son of God, the bride, the Lamb's wife, the completeness of Him who fills all in all."[2] "The mystical universal church is His [Christ's] body as the Israelitish church is the body of Moses."[3] And "it is the glory of the church of Christ, that she, in all her members...is thus one, one holy society, one city, one family."[4] We also must remember that "the church of Christ is a school appointed for the training up Christ's little children, to greater degrees of knowledge, higher privileges, and greater serviceableness in this world, and more of the meetness for the possession of their eternal inheritance."[5]

Your view would be in accordance with the Westminster Confession of Faith *(19:3) that Old Testament Israel was "a church under age."*

JE: Yes, the church at that time was as "in a child's state."[6] "The church, under the Old Testament, was a child under tutors and governors, and God dealt with it accordingly. Those pompous externals are called by the apostle, weak and beggarly elements."[7] The "state of things" under the Old Testament "was a typical state of things, and that not only the ceremonies of the law were typical, but that their [the Israelites'] history and constitution of the nation and their state and circumstances were typical. It was, as it were, a typical world." All of these "were typical of things appertaining to the Messiah and His church and kingdom."[8] "The church of the Jews is called the body of Moses, as the Christian church is called the body of Christ. Moses was herein a type of Christ."[9]

Yet, there is only one true church from the beginning of time until the end of time.

JE: That is correct. "Those that are saints now, they are of the same church with the apostles, and with David and Samuel and Moses, and Abraham, Isaac, and Jacob. They are all but one church."[10]

We know that a goodly number of persons in Old Testament Israel, even though in the church, fell away. Which was the most faithful generation?

JE: "There was a remarkable outpouring of the Spirit of God on the children of Israel in the wilderness, on the younger generation, their little ones that they said should be a prey, the generation that entered into Canaan with Joshua.... That generation seems to have been the most excellent generation that ever was in the church of Israel. There is no generation of which there is so much good and so little hurt spoken in Scripture."[11]

Where is the gospel most clearly set forth in the Old Testament?

JE: In "the prophet Isaiah, gospel light is fullest and clearest of all, beyond what we have in any other Old Testament revelation."[12]

The Bible speaks of Christ as the husband of the church.

JE: Yes, it does. By agreement within the Trinity, Christ is the "husband and vital head of the church."[13]

In Ephesians 1, Paul speaks of the church as the completeness of Christ. What does this mean?

JE: "The church is said to be the completeness of Christ (Ephesians 1:23), as if Christ were not complete without the church, as having a natural inclination thereto. We are incomplete without that which we have a natural inclination to. Thus, man is incomplete without the woman, she is himself; so Christ is not complete without His spouse."[14]

Within the visible church, of course, there is always a mixture of believers and unbelievers; isn't this correct?

JE: Certainly, this is correct. "The visible church is made up of true and false Christians."[15] As I told my own congregation, "I do verily think that there are a number of people belonging to this congregation in imminent danger of being damned to all eternity."[16] And "those who are truly converted are visible only to God."[17] "They [who] at the day of judgment shall be found not to have been faithful, that have not persevered. They shall be rejected and cast out of Christ's church and out of God's house. Such branches shall be cut off from the vine." Such persons were never truly in the invisible "church of Christ or house of God," nor were they ever true branches "in the true vine."[18]

It is the case, then, that there may be a goodly number of hypocrites in the church?

JE: Indeed so. Scripture makes it clear that "very often those pass among them [church members] for saints, and it may be eminent saints, that are grand hypocrites."[19]

It is common among theologians to distinguish between the church triumphant and the church militant. Is this proper?

JE: Yes, it is, but "let it be considered that the church on earth is the same society with those saints who are praising God in heaven. There is not one church of Christ in heaven and the other here upon the earth. Though the one is sometimes called 'the church triumphant,' and the other 'the church militant,' yet they are not indeed two churches. By the 'church triumphant' is meant the triumphant part of the church [in heaven], and by 'the church militant' the militant part of it [on earth]; for there is but one universal, catholic church."[20] Or said another way, "the church militant is Christ's army; they go forth with Christ, and under Christ, to fight the good fight of faith, and are soldiers of Jesus Christ." Yet at the same time "when God is doing some great thing for His church on earth, the hosts of heaven are engaged with the church on earth."[21]

Does the church triumphant, then, understand or witness that which is taking place on earth with the church militant?

JE: Oh yes. "The saints [in heaven] are spectators of God's providence relating to the church here below." There is biblical evidence to show "that the saints in heaven are acquainted with the affairs of the church here on earth, and also that a considerable part of their happiness consists in seeing the dispensations and works of God's grace towards the church on earth, and the discovering of His glory therein."[22]

In the Westminster Confession of Faith *(26:1) we read about the church and "the communion of the saints." The Westminster Assembly teaches that all of the saints are united to Christ as their Head, and therefore there is a union that they have with one another. Is this your view?*

JE: It is. "Though many individual persons were chosen [by God], yet they were chosen to receive God's infinite and peculiar love in union as one body, one spouse, all united in one Head [Christ]."[23] And the Holy Spirit "is the bond of perfectness by which God, Jesus Christ and the church are united together."[24]

What about the responsibility of Christians, both individually and corporately (as a church body) to live at peace with one another?

JE: "It is an indispensable duty incumbent upon us to endeavor, to the utmost of our power, to live peaceably with all men." This is a duty for the church with regard to "unjust and sinful men as well as with those who are to appearances true Christians and the fearers of God." Those members of the church who "are not of a peaceable temper are not in a state of salvation."[25]

What form of church government do you consider to be the most biblical?

JE: I agree with the Westminster Standards, that "the Presbyterian [form of church] government" is the one "most agreeable to the Word of God."[26]

Then even though you have ministered in congregational churches, you are not a strict congregationalist? You believe, for instance, in church councils.

JE: I am not a "strict" congregationalist. "It is the mind of God that not a mixed multitude but only select persons of distinguished ability and integrity are fit for the business of judging causes."[27] Furthermore, "it is unreasonable to suppose, that there is no cause can arise in the church too hard for a particular minister or a particular congregation, and that there should be no need in no case of an resort, or appeal, or referring of the cause to a higher judgment."[28] The "institution of ecclesiastical councils…[is] for ordering the affairs of the church of Christ."[29]

We know that with all things, the ecclesiastical censure of "excommunication" is to be carried out for the glory of God. But what are the "ends" of this censure?

JE: First, we need to understand that "those members of the visible church who are become visibly wicked, ought not to be tolerated in the church, but should be excommunicated." But "the special ends of it are these three: First, that the church be kept pure, and the ordinances of God not be defiled.... Second, that others may be deterred from wickedness. As the neglect of proper censure, with respect to visibly wicked church members, tends to lead and encourage others to commit the same wickedness, so the infliction of proper censure tends to restrain others not only from the same wickedness, but from sin in general.... Third, that the persons themselves may be reclaimed, and their souls may be saved."[30]

We are to understand that that is a very serious censure; is this correct?

JE: Yes. "They that are regularly and justly excommunicated, they are bound in heaven; the wrath of God abides upon them. While they justly stand excommunicated, they ordinarily stand bound to damnation. I say ordinarily, because it is possible that the case may be so, that they may desire to do what is proper to be restored, and may not have opportunity.... So that excommunication does as much mark out men as being in a damnable condition, as if it made them so [without repentance and restoration]."[31]

The Reformed church has always held to what is called the "regulative principle" of worship, which maintains that God is only to be worshipped as commanded, either explicitly or implicitly, in His Word. Is this your view as well?

JE: Yes, it is. "Nothing is to be done in the worship of God more or less but what God has instituted."[32] This can be seen in the differences between Martha and Mary, as found in Luke 10:38-42. "Martha and Mary seem to be types of different churches, or rather different parts of the Christian church: the one showing their respect to Christ by much external service and ceremony, as Martha was cumbered about much serving; the other that part of the church that is more pure and spiritual in their worship, as Mary sat at His feet, and heard His Word.... Mary represents...[those] who worship

Christ according to His institutions, without the pomp and cumbrance of outward forms.... Christ declares that Mary's way of showing respect to Him was far the most necessary and most acceptable; so is that worship that is pure and spiritual."[33] We must be sure that "the main thing that we prize in God's house be not the outward ornaments of it, or a high seat in it, but the Word of God and His ordinances."[34] "If any ceremonies in divine worship are in any wise unlawful for this reason, because they are ceremonies of human invention, then human invention is a thing that makes ceremonies unlawful in the worship of God."[35] This principle is also taught in Leviticus 10, where Nadab and Abihu "took upon them to begin and introduce a service into religion which was not appointed, they offered what the Lord commanded them not; and this, if it had been suffered [permitted], would have opened a door to great irregularities, and the Jewish religion would in a little time have been, not what God had directed, but would have abounded in many human inventions added to it."[36]

Tell us about the use of the "imprecatory" Psalms.

JE: "It is not unlawful for the people of God...to pray that God would appear on their side, and plead and vindicate their cause, and punish those wicked men that are entirely and impenitently and implacably their enemies, in a righteous cause.... Especially it is not unsuitable thus to pray against our enemies, if the cause wherein they are our enemies is the cause of God."[37] "We cannot think that those imprecations we find in the Psalms and Prophets were out of their own hearts." Rather, "they wish them ill, not as personal, but as public, enemies to the church of God."[38]

From what you have said, and from your various writings, you seem to have a great love for singing and music.

JE: Yes, "singing is amiable, because of the proportion that is perceived in it; singing in divine worship is beautiful and useful, because it expresses and promotes the harmonious exercise of the mind. There will doubtless, in the future world, be that which, as it will be an expression of an immensely greater and more excellent harmony of the mind, so will be a far more lively expression of this harmony [of singing]; and shall itself be vastly more harmonious, yea, than our air or ears, by any modulation, is capable of."[39] "The best, most beautiful, and most perfect way that we have of expressing a sweet concord of mind to each other, is by music. When I would form in my mind an idea of a society in the highest degree happy, I think of them as expressing their love, their joy, and the inward concord and harmony and spiritual beauty of their souls by sweetly singing to each other." And with regard to "the glorified saints, after they have again received their bodies," they will make music; "and the music they will make will be in a medium capable of modulations in an infinitely more nice, exact and fine proportion than our gross air, and with organs as much more adapted to such proportions."[40]

How many New Testament sacraments are there?

JE: Two: baptism and the Lord's supper. In Matthew 28:19-20 we have "an appointment of Christian baptism. This ordinance indeed had a beginning before; John the Baptist and Christ [both baptized]. But now, especially by this institution, is it established as an ordinance to be upheld in the Christian church to the end of the world. The ordinance of the Lord's supper had been established before [Luke 22:14-20]."[41]

Augustine taught that the sacraments function as visible words. Do you agree?

JE: I do. God "has not only appointed that we should be told the great things of the gospel, and of the redemption of Christ, and instructed in them by His Word; but also that they should be, as it were, exhibited to our view, in sensible representations, in the sacraments, the more to affect them to us."[42]

Are there not two sides (God's side and man's side) to the sacraments, which sacraments are signs and seals of the covenant of grace?

JE: Yes, there are. "The sacraments are not only seals of the offer on God's part, or ordinances God has appointed as confirmations of the truth of His covenant." But "a man can have no right to them without a compliance with the terms." "It is not reasonable to suppose, that the seal of the covenant belongs to any man, as a party in the covenant, who will not accept of and comply with the covenant."[43]

You do not believe that grace is conveyed by the sacraments ex opere operato *("by the work performed"), do you?*

JE: Definitely not; "the sacraments have no effect but by the Word [of God]."[44]

You are an adherent of infant baptism. Do you see this as a covenantal requirement coming from the Old Testament into the New?

JE: Yes. "Far am I from thinking the Old Testament to be like an old almanac out of use; nay, I think it is evident from the New Testament that some things, which had their first institution under the Old Testament, are continued under the New; for instance, the acceptance of the infant-seed of believers as children of the covenant with their parents."[45]

Do you agree with the Westminster Confession of Faith *(28:3) that "dipping of the person into the water is not necessary; but baptism is rightly administered by pouring, or sprinkling water upon the person?"*

JE: Yes. "Baptism by sprinkling" (or "pouring") is "a more lively representation of the thing signified by baptism than dipping or plunging."[46]

How is the ordinance of baptism efficacious, then, to the infant-seed?

JE: "If an adult person does sincerely and believingly dedicate the infant to God baptism seals salvation to it.... So if a parent did sincerely and with his whole heart dedicate his child to God, he will afterward take thorough and effectual care in bringing up his children in the nurture and admonition of the Lord, continuing in prayer and dependence on God for them; and in that way it is sealed to them, that ordinarily they shall obtain success."[47]

What about the baptized infants of believing parents who die in infancy; are they saved?

JE: "If the parents do sincerely, believingly, and entirely, with a thorough disposition, will and desire, dedicate their child to God that they bring to baptism, if that child dies in infancy, the parents have good grounds to hope for its salvation."[48]

What is the Lord's supper?

JE: The Lord's supper serves as "a kind of visible Word.... [God] made the gospel visible in this ordinance."[49] "The Lord's supper is a feast appointed to signify and seal Christians' union with Christ and one to another."[50] It is "the Christian church's great feast of love; wherein Christ's people sit together as brethren in the family of God, at their Father's table, to feast on the love of their Redeemer...sealing their love to Him and one another."[51] "We who are professing Christians are under solemn vows and engagements to be the Lord's and to serve Him. Every time we come to the Lord's Supper we renew those vows in a most solemn manner."[52] The Lord's Supper "was appointed to draw forth the longings of our souls towards Jesus Christ. Here are the glorious objects of spiritual desire by visible signs represented to our view. We have Christ evidently set forth as crucified. Here we have that spiritual meat and drink represented and offered to excite our hunger and thirst; here we have all that spiritual feast represented which God has provided for poor souls; and here we may hope in some measure to have our longing souls satisfied in this world by the gracious communications of the Spirit of God."[53]

Are you saying that there is a memorial aspect to the Lord's supper?

JE: Yes, Christ said "this do in remembrance of Me." It is a "representation...of His dying love to us." Herein we "keep alive the memory of the cross of Christ."[54]

But it is also more than this.

JE: That is correct. It is a means of grace, a "gospel provision...fitly represented by a feast because it nourishes the soul as food."[55]

What is the efficacy of the Lord's supper?

JE: The believer feeds on Christ. It "is the communion of Christians in the body and blood of Christ." "All divine blessings are as much in and through Christ as if they were a feast provided of His flesh that was given for us." "Those that spiritually partake of Christ they eat angel's food."[56] Partaking of the Lord's supper makes the soul to "grow as food does the body." In this communion, "our souls are united to the person of Jesus in beholding His excellencies and glory." Christians partake of "the excellencies of the person of Christ and His love [which] are their food."[57]

So in the Lord's supper there is a "present" aspect involved as well, i.e., we commune with Him in the present.

JE: Precisely. "The saints have communion with Christ in glory now [at the Lord's supper] and shall partake of the same glory in heaven."[58]

You do not believe that at the Lord's supper the communicants partake of the actual body and blood of Christ?

JE: No; to me this would be "a thing so horrid and monstrous as the Papists do in their doctrine of transubstantiation."[59]

But Christ is truly present at the Lord's supper?

JE: Yes. As Christ was "bodily present" at the first Lord's supper, He is spiritually present with us now so that we "may look upon Him as sitting with [us] at His table."[60] Christ was "not only [present] with His disciples at the first sacrament, but He sits with His people in every sacrament."[61] At the Lord's supper, "there is a [spiritual] presence of Christ by special manifestation of Himself and tokens of His presence whereby Christ may be said to be present with Christians and not all others."[62]

From what you said about the Roman Catholic Church's false view of the sacraments, do you mean that the sacraments of the Roman Church are not to be considered as valid sacraments?

JE: The "sacraments of the church of Rome" are "spurious."[63]

Who should be admitted to the Lord's supper?

JE: Those who come to the Supper "must be Christians really," and they must "examine and prove themselves, whether or not they believe the gospel with all their hearts, or are heartily convinced of the truth of it."[64] "It is the mind and will of God that none should be admitted to full communion in the church of Christ but such as in profession and in the eye of a reasonable judgment are truly saints or godly persons."[65] We must remember that at the Lord's supper we "openly own and renew the covenant of grace," and we offer ourselves "to God to be His in an everlasting covenant and cleave to Him and to His people."[66]

What does such a profession of faith entail?

JE: "A public profession of [the Christian] religion has respect to two things. It has respect to something present, *viz.* their belief of faith. This is the profession God's people make of their faith. And it has respect to something future, *viz.* their future behavior in the promises or vows that are made in a public profession."[67]

When you talk about self-examination before coming to the Lord's supper, what are you referring to?

JE: In a sermon on 1 Corinthians 11:28-29, I summarized the process of self-examination as follows: Before coming to the Lord's supper, persons should examine themselves as to: 1) whether they are living "habitually…[in] any known sin," even sins "against the habitual light of [their] conscience"; 2) as to "whether or no it be their serious resolution to avoid all sin and live in obedience to all known commands [of God]"; 3) as to whether or not "they entertain a spirit of hatred or envy or revenge towards their neighbor"; 4) as to "what it is they aim at in coming to the Lord's supper." Is it for their "spiritual good…[with a] regard to God's command," or simply for "temporal advantage or credit," and/or false pretense.[68]

Is the Lord's supper to be viewed as a kind of "confirmation?"

JE: Yes. "Confirmation is undoubtedly a gospel institution. And sacrament too; and it is the sacrament of the Lord's Supper: that is the confirmation that Christ has instituted. Children, as soon as ever they are capable of it, should come and publicly make what was done in their baptism their own act by partaking of the Lord's Supper."[69]

Some have accused you of teaching that only those who you determine are truly converted should come to the Lord's supper. How would you respond to this accusation?

JE: No, this is not my view. Rather, "it is a credible profession and visibility of these things [godly actions], that is the church's rule in this case."[70] "I am far from pretending to a discriminating judgment of men's spiritual state, so as infallibly to determine who are true converts and who are not, or imagining that I, or anybody else is sufficient for the execution of any such design as the setting up a pure church consisting only of true converts."[71]

Would your view on this subject, perhaps, keep some truly godly persons away from the Lord's supper?

JE: Perhaps so, but "is it not better, that some true saints, through their own weakness and misunderstanding, should be kept away from the Lord's Table, which will not keep such out of heaven; than voluntarily to bring in multitudes of false professors to partake unworthily, and in effect to seal their own condemnation?"[72]

One question that frequently rises has to do with Judas Iscariot. Did he take the Lord's supper in the upper room with Jesus Christ?

JE: "It is to me apparent, that Judas was not present at the administration of the Lord's supper."[73]

How often should the Lord's supper be administered?

JE: Weekly. "Christ's institutions" calls for "the administration of the Lord's supper every Lord's Day."[74]

We have already talked about the use of the means of grace and their importance in the process of sanctification. You consider them indispensable.

JE: I do. "God's Spirit always attends His ordinances."[75] "All the stated means of grace" were established "in the apostolic age…and are to remain unaltered to the day of judgment."[76] God's kingdom advances on earth (individually and corporately) not by extraordinary means, but "by the preaching of the gospel, and the use of the ordinary means of grace."[77]

How do the means of grace function?

JE: "The means of grace, such as the Word and sacraments, supply the mind with notions, or speculative ideas, of the things of religion, and thus give an opportunity for grace to act in the soul; for hereby the soul is supplied with matter for grace to act upon, when God is pleased to infuse it…. The more fully we are supplied with these notions, the greater opportunity has grace to act.... Here therefore, is the benefit of frequent and abundant instructions; here is the benefit of study and mediation, and comparing spiritual things with spiritual.... The oftener these notions or ideas are revived, and the more they are upheld in the soul, the greater opportunity for the Spirit of God to infuse grace.... By what has been said, we see the necessity of means of grace in order to the obtaining grace; for without means there could be no opportunity for grace to act.... Neither will God give grace, where there is no opportunity for it to act."[78]

To take this a step further, I see the pool of Bethesda (John 5:1ff.) as a "type and representation of gospel ordinances and means of grace, and the way that persons are to seek spiritual healing by them." The ordinances heal or save by "supernatural influence," not by any virtue in the ordinances themselves. It is God who "gives the influences of His Spirit" when He is pleased to do so.[79]

The Reformers in general believed that the Antichrist is the Roman Catholic papacy. What is your view?

JE: I agree. "The rise of the Antichrist was gradual... [with] the bishop of Rome gradually assuming more and more authority to himself...then afterwards he claimed the authority of universal bishop over the whole Christian church through the world.... Till at length he, [allegedly] as Christ's vicar on earth, claimed the very same power that Christ would have if He was presently on earth."[80] The pope "sets himself up as universal king of the church in His [Christ's] room, and usurps His throne."[81] "Their [the papacy's] whole religion is blasphemy."[82] "Popery is the deepest contrivance that ever Satan was the author of to uphold his kingdom."[83]

How will the Antichrist be overthrown?

JE: "We know that Antichrist is to be destroyed by clear

light, by the breath of Christ's mouth…[by] the Word of God, and the clear light of the gospel."[84]

But you also claim that Islam is a very dangerous anti-Christian religion, do you not?

JE: Very definitely so. Roman Catholicism and Islam "are the two great works of the devil that he in this space of time wrought against the kingdom of Christ." Islam is a "great kingdom of mighty power and vast extent that Satan set up against the kingdom of Christ. He set this up in the eastern empire as he did Antichrist [Roman Catholicism] in the western."[85] Whereas "Christianity was propagated by light, instruction, and knowledge…by the gospel," Islam was propagated by "darkness," and it "was propagated by the sword also," and it was propagated "by an ignorant and barbarous sort of people." Islam is a religion "suited to the desires of the flesh, and to the allurements of the world." Some of its teachings "are too childish and ridiculous to be publicly mentioned in solemn assembly." Islam is "a gross delusion."[86]

From early on in the Christian church, Sunday has been the Christian Sabbath. Why is this so?

JE: "Even though this [the Christian Sabbath] was gradually established in the Christian church, yet those things by which the revelation of God's mind and will was made began on the day of Christ's resurrection, by His then appearing to His disciples [John 20:19], and was then afterwards confirmed by His appearing from time to time on that day rather than any other day [John 20:26], and His sending down the Holy Spirit so remarkably on that day [Acts 2:1-4], and afterwards in directing that the public assemblies and public worship of Christians should be on that day [Acts 20:7; 1 Corinthians 16:1-2; Revelation 1:10]. And so the day of the week on which Christ rose from the dead, that joyful day, is appointed to be the day of the church's holy rejoicing to the end of the world, and the day of their stated public worship.

And this is a very great and principal means of the success that the gospel has had in the world."[87] "So that since the Lord has been pleased to call the first day of the week by His name (Revelation 1:10), we may conclude that this is the day that the Lord has blessed and hallowed; and therefore that He has appointed this day to be kept as a sabbath, holy unto Himself (Genesis 2:3)."[88] It is the "Lord's Day."[89]

I believe it is also your view that Sunday, the first day of the week was Adam's Sabbath day as well.

JE: That is correct. "This first Sabbath being the first day of Adam's life, and so the first day from whence he began to reckon time, was the first day of his week; and so, that the first day of the week was the day that God sanctified to be kept by all nations and ages, excepting the change that was made of the day of the Sabbath for the Israelitish nation after coming out of Egypt, till the resurrection of Christ."[90]

Let me ask you about church officers. How many offices are there in the church of Christ?

JE: Two; ministers (teaching elders) and deacons. And these "offices that Christ has appointed in His church do respect either the souls or bodies of men."[91]

What are the duties of the minister?

JE: "The work of ministers is very often in the New Testament compared to the business of the husbandmen [farmers] that take care of God's husbandry...ministers are called laborers in God's harvest...so the work of a minister is very often in Scripture represented by the business of a shepherd or pastor."[92] "A minister by his office is to be a guide and instructor of his people. To this end he is to study and search the Scriptures and to teach the people—not the opinions of men, of other divines or of their ancestors, but the mind of Christ."[93]

Does the minister take vows to this end?

JE: Yes, he does. "It was implied in my [own] ordination vows that I would study the Scriptures; that I would make the Word of God, and not the word of any man, my rule in teaching my people; and that I would do my utmost to know what was the counsel of God, and to declare it."[94]

You most obviously believe that the pastor of a congregation has a very important role to play in the spiritual lives of his congregation. What sort of man should he be?

JE: "It is the excellency of a minister of the gospel to be both a burning and shining light.... If a minister has light without heat, and entertains his auditory with learned discourses, without a savor of the power of godliness, or an appearance of fervency, of spirit, and zeal for God and the good of souls, he may gratify itching ears, and fill the heads of his people with empty notions; but it will not be very likely to reach their hearts, or save their souls. And if, on the other hand, he be driven on with a fierce and intemperate zeal, and vehement heat, without light, he will be likely to kindle the like unhallowed flame in his people, and to fire their corrupt passions and affections; but will make them never the better, nor lead them a step toward heaven, but drive them apace the other way.... But if he approves himself in his ministry, as both a burning and shining light, this will be the way to promote true Christianity amongst his people, and to make them both wise and good, and cause religion to flourish among them in the purity and beauty of it." It is also the case that ministers, "in order to be burning and shining lights, should walk closely with God, and keep near to Christ; that they may ever be enlightened and enkindled by Him. And they should be much in seeking God, and conversing with Him by prayer, who is the fountain of light and love."[95]

What is the responsibility of the congregation to the pastor?

JE: Just "as the bridegroom and the bride give themselves

to each other in covenant, so it is in that union…between a faithful pastor and a Christian people." The congregation is responsible "to love and honor him [the pastor], and willingly submit [themselves] to him, as a virgin when married to an husband." In "rejecting him," they "will reject Christ."[96] It is also the duty of the congregation financially to support their pastor. It has "been a thing established from the beginning of the world, that God's visible people [the church] should offer a part of their substance to God" to provide "for them that dwell before the Lord, to eat sufficiently, and for durable clothing."[97]

What is the job of the deacons?

JE: "The appointment of the office of deacons in the Christian church, which we [first] have an account of in the sixth chapter of the Acts, [is] to take care for the outward supply of the members of Christ's church, and the exercise of that great Christian virtue of charity."[98] That is, "the main business of a deacon by Christ's appointments is to take care of the distribution of the church's charity, for the outward supply of those in need."[99]

Christian charity, then, is a necessary part of the church.

JE: "It is the absolute and indispensable duty of the people of God to give bountifully and willingly for the supply of the wants of the needy."[100] "The Scripture is as plain as it is possible that it should be, that none are true saints, but those whose true character it is, that they are of a disposition to pity and relieve their fellow creatures, that are poor, indigent, and afflicted."[101]

From what you have said, it is the Christian's duty to tithe.

JE: Yes, as I stated above, from the very beginning of the church, "God's visible people" are called upon to "offer a part of their substance to God…. And this duty does not cease with the abolition of the Mosaic dispensation. There is nothing that argues that now a less proportion of what we have should be offered to God than formerly, but the Scripture seems rather to intimate that, in gospel [New Testament] times, God's people should consecrate more of their substance to God."[102]

Finally, on this subject, I would ask you to comment on the relationship between church and state.

JE: I basically agree with chapter 23 of the *Westminster Confession of Faith:* "The civil authorities having nothing to do with matters ecclesiastical, with those things which relate to conscience and eternal salvation or with any matter religious as religious, is reconcilable still with their having to do with some matters that, in some sense, concern religion. For although they have to do with nothing but civil affairs, and although their business extends no further than the civil interests of the people, yet by reason of the profession of religion and the difference that matters religious make in the state and circumstances of a people, many things become civil which otherwise would not. Now by the civil interests or advantages of a people…I think is commonly meant their general interest or their interest as they are a people in this world, whether it [be] their general profit or pleasure or peace or honor."[103]

Is it ever proper for the Christian to defend himself, and for the civil magistrate to fight a just war in defense of the community?

JE: Yes on both accounts. Christians may have "to defend and vindicate themselves, though it be to the damage of him who injures them."[104] And there is certainly a time when "a people of God may be called to go forth to war," because "if it be lawful for a particular person to defend himself with force, then it is lawful for a nation of people made up of persons" to do the same.[105]

Is there a place for a conscientious objector when it comes to going to war?

JE: Yes, if it "be notoriously manifest that the war is unjust."[106]

---

[1] Edwards, *Sermon* on 1 Peter 2:9.
[2] Edwards, *Miscellany* 103.
[3] Edwards, *Sermon* on Numbers 11:10-15.
[4] Edwards, *Sermon* on Luke 6:35.
[5] Edwards, *Works* (Yale), 12:264.
[6] Edwards, *Miscellany* 1354.
[7] Edwards, *Works*, I:558.
[8] Edwards, *Works* (Yale), 11:146, 320.
[9] Edwards, *Works* (Yale), 15:80.
[10] Edwards, *Sermon* on Ephesians 5:25-27.
[11] Edwards, *Works* (Yale), 4:504.
[12] Edwards, *Works* (Yale), 15:228.
[13] Edwards, *Miscellany* 1062.
[14] Edwards, *Miscellany* 104.
[15] Edwards, *Sermon* on Matthew 25:12.
[16] Edwards, *Sermon* on Isaiah 61:2.
[17] Edwards, *Sermon* on Psalm 55:12-14.
[18] Edwards, *Miscellany* 722.
[19] Edwards, *Works*, I:cci.
[20] Edwards, *Sermon* on Revelation 14:2.
[21] Edwards, *Works* (Yale), 15:131-132.
[22] Edwards, *Works* (Yale), 18:99.
[23] Edwards, *Miscellany* 1245.
[24] Edwards, *Miscellany* 487.
[25] Edwards, *Sermon* on Romans 12:18.
[26] Edwards, *Works* (Yale), 16:355.
[27] Edwards, *Sermon* on Deuteronomy 1:13-18.
[28] Edwards, *Miscellany* 349.
[29] Edwards, *Works* (Yale), 9:368.
[30] Edwards, *Sermon* on 1 Corinthians 5:11.
[31] Edwards, *Miscellany* 485.
[32] Edwards, *Miscellany* 76.
[33] Edwards, *Works*, II:789.
[34] Cited in *Our Great and Glorious God*, 212.
[35] Edwards, *Miscellany* 12.
[36] Edwards, *Miscellany* 1088.
[37] Edwards, *Miscellany* 640.
[38] Edwards, *Works*, II:465-466.

[39] Edwards, *Miscellany* 153.
[40] Edwards, *Miscellany* 188.
[41] Edwards, *Works* (Yale), 9:364.
[42] Edwards, *Works* (Yale), 2:115.
[43] Edwards, *Works* (Yale), 12:413.
[44] Edwards, *Works*, II:264.
[45] Edwards, *Works*, I:465.
[46] Edwards, *Miscellany* 694.
[47] Edwards, *Miscellany* 595.
[48] Edwards, *Miscellany* 577.
[49] Edwards, *Sermon* on 1 Corinthians 10:16.
[50] Edwards, *Sermon* on 1 Corinthians 10:17.
[51] Edwards, *Works* (Yale), 12:255.
[52] Edwards, *Sermon* on Hosea 11:9.
[53] Edwards, *Sermon* on Song of Solomon 5:1.
[54] Edwards, *Sermon* on Luke 22:19.
[55] Edwards, *Sermon* on Luke 14:16.
[56] Cited in Gerstner, *The Rational Biblical Theology of Jonathan Edwards*, III:446.
[57] Edwards, *Sermon* on 1 Corinthians 10:16.
[58] Edwards, *Sermon* on 1 Corinthians 1:9.
[59] Edwards, *Sermon* on 1 Corinthians 10:16.
[60] Edwards, *Sermon* on 1 Corinthians 10:16.
[61] Edwards, *Sermon* on Luke 14:16.
[62] Edwards, *Sermon* on Matthew 9:15.
[63] Edwards, *Works* (Yale), 12:497.
[64] Edwards, *Miscellany* 462.
[65] Edwards, *Sermon* on Ezekiel 44:9.
[66] Edwards, *Sermon* on 1 Corinthians 10:16.
[67] Edwards, *Works* (Yale), 15:556.
[68] Cited in William J. Danaher, Jr., "By Sensible Signs Represented," *Pro Ecclesia* (Vol. VII, No. 3), 281-282.
[69] Edwards, *Miscellany* 207.
[70] Edwards, *Works*, I:434-435.
[71] Edwards, *Works* (Yale), 16:343.
[72] Edwards, *Works* (Yale), 12:310.
[73] Edwards, *Works* (Yale), 12:288.
[74] Edwards, *Works* (Yale), 16:366.
[75] Edwards, *Works*, I:539.
[76] Edwards, *Works* (Yale), 9:370.
[77] Edwards, *Works* (Yale), 9:459.
[78] Edwards, *Miscellany* 539.
[79] Edwards, *Works* (Yale), 15:532.
[80] Edwards, *Works* (Yale), 9:412.
[81] Edwards, *Miscellany* 340.

[82] Edwards, *Works* (Yale), 5:125-126.
[83] Edwards, *Works* (Yale), 5:119.
[84] Edwards, *Works* (Yale), 5:118.
[85] Edwards, *Works* (Yale), 9:410, 415.
[86] Edwards, *Works*, II:492-493.
[87] Edwards, *Works* (Yale), 9:363.
[88] Edwards, *Miscellany* 536.
[89] Edwards, *Miscellany* 495.
[90] Cited in Grosart, *Selections From the Unpublished Writings of Jonathan Edwards*, 59.
[91] Edwards, *Sermon* on Romans 12:4.
[92] Edwards, *Works* (Yale), 4:434.
[93] Edwards, *Works* (Yale), 12:559.
[94] Edwards, *Works* (Yale), 12:565.
[95] Edwards, *Sermon* on John 5:35.
[96] Cited in Scheick, *The Writings of Jonathan Edwards*, 114-115.
[97] Edwards, *Miscellany* 850.
[98] Edwards, *Works* (Yale), 9:367.
[99] Edwards, *Works* (Yale), 18:501.
[100] Edwards, *Sermon* on Deuteronomy 15:7-11.
[101] Edwards, *Works* (Yale), 2:355.
[102] Edwards, *Miscellany* 850.
[103] Edwards, *Miscellany* 14.
[104] Edwards, *Works* 8:191-192.
[105] Edwards, *Sermon* on 1 Kings 8:44-45.
[106] Edwards, *Sermon* on Nehemiah 4:14.

CHAPTER 10

Edwards on the Family

Tell us something about the husband-wife relationship, as given to us in the Word of God.

JE: "Now it is easy for everyone to know that when a marriage is according to nature and God's designation, when a woman is married to an husband she receives him as a guide, as a protector, a safeguard and defense, a shelter from harms and dangers, a reliever from distresses, a comforter in afflictions, a support in discouragements. God has so designed it, and therefore has made man of a more robust [nature], and strong in body and mind, with more wisdom, strength, and courage, fit to protect and defend; but he has made woman weaker, more soft and tender, more fearful, and more affectionate, as a fit object of generous protection and defense.... Thus it is against nature for a man to love a woman as wife that is rugged, daring, and presumptuous, and trusts in herself and needs none of her husband's defense or guidance. And it is impossible a woman should love a man as an husband, except she can confide in him, and sweetly rest in him as a safeguard."[1]

What about family order?

JE: Parents are over their children, and "the relation of a natural parent brings great obligations on children." And "let children obey their parents, and yield to their instructions, and submit to their orders, as they would inherit a blessing and not a curse. For we have reason to think, from many things in the Word of God, that nothing has a greater tendency to bring a curse on persons in this world, and on all their temporal concerns, than undutiful, unsubmissive, disorderly behavior in children toward their parents."[2]

How do you view the Christian family, and the education of children?

JE: "Every Christian family ought to be as it were a little church, consecrated to Christ, and wholly influenced and governed by His rules. And family education and order are some of the chief of the means of grace."[3] Young children within a Christian family are "the very best field for evangelism." "Persons when in their youth are ordinarily more easily awakened than afterward. Their minds are tender and it is a more easy thing to make impression upon them."[4]

Why is it that we see so many children within Christian families falling away from the Christian faith?

JE: I believe that "it is very much owing to parents, that there are so many young people who can make no profession of godliness: they have themselves therefore to blame.... If ancestors had thoroughly done their duty to their posterity in instructing, praying for, and governing their children, and setting good examples, there is reason to think, the case would have been far otherwise."[5]

---

[1] Edwards, *Miscellany* 37.

[2] Edwards, *Sermon* on 2 Corinthians 1:14.

[3] Edwards, *Sermon* on 2 Corinthians 1:14.

[4] Edwards, *Sermon* on Job 20:11.

[5] Edwards, *Works* (Yale), 12:315.

CHAPTER 11
Edwards on Eschatology

In your doctrine of the last things, you are known as a postmillennialist.

JE: Yes, there will be a time when "there shall be a glorious pouring out of the Spirit with this clear and powerful preaching of the gospel, to make it successful for reviving those holy doctrines of religion that are now chiefly ridiculed in the world, and turning multitudes from heresy, and from popery, and from other false religion, and also for turning many from their vice and profaneness, and for bringing vast multitudes savingly home to Christ."[1] "How happy will that state be…when the distant extremes of the world shall shake hands together and all nations shall be acquainted, and they shall all join the forces of their minds in exploring the glories of their Creator, their hearts in loving and adoring Him, their hands in serving Him, and their voices in making the world to ring with His praise."[2] This will be "the time of the church's latter day glory."[3] And "the day of the commencement of the church's latter day glory is eminently the day of Christ's espousals, when as the bridegroom rejoices over the bride, so He will rejoice over His church."[4] This "will be a time wherein [Christian] religion shall in every respect be uppermost in the world. It shall be in great esteem and honor. The saints have hitherto for the most part been kept under, and wicked men have governed. But now they will be uppermost."[5] "There was indeed a glorious season of the application of redemption, in the first ages of the Christian church, that began at Jerusalem, on the Day of Pentecost; but that was not the proper time of ingathering; it was only as it were the Feast of First Fruits; the ingathering is at the end of the year, or in the last ages of the Christian church…and will probably as much exceed what was in the first ages of the Christian church, though that filled the Roman Empire, as that exceeded all that had been before, under the Old Testament, confined only to the land of Judea."[6]

This is the millennium that theologians talk about; correct?

JE: Yes. In this "millennium…there are remaining glorious times of the church."[7] "I think…it is probable that there will be an hundred thousand times more, that will actually be redeemed to God by Christ's blood, during that period of the church's prosperity that we have been speaking of [the millennium], than ever had been before, from the beginning of the world to that time."[8] I would say that during this time "there will probably be an hundred times more of the application of redemption than in all preceding ages put together."[9] "God has suffered many earthly princes to extend their conquests over a great part of the face of the earth, and to possess a dominion of vast extent, and one monarchy to conquer and succeed another, the latter being still the greater: it is reasonable to suppose that a much greater glory in this respect should be reserved for Christ, God's own Son and rightful heir, who has purchased the dominion by so great and hard a service: it is reasonable to suppose, that His dominion should be far the largest, and His conquests vastly the greatest and most extensive…. And thus it is meet, that the last kingdom which shall take place on earth, should be the kingdom of God's own Son and heir, whose right it is to rule and reign."[10] At this time, "the whole earth shall become more sensibly, as it were, one family, one holy and happy society."[11]

Is this the time that we read about in Romans 11?

JE: Yes, it is. "Nothing is more certainly foretold than this national conversion of the Jews in Romans 11.... Though we do not know the time in which this conversion of Israel will come to pass; yet thus much we may determine by Scripture, that it will be before the glory of the Gentile part of the church shall be fully accomplished; because it is said, that their coming in shall be life from the dead to the Gentiles."[12]

What does the Lord of the church have to say about the millennium?

JE: In Matthew 28:18-19, we see that "it was Christ's aim to assert His right over mankind that He had acquired by the labors He went through...and therefore inasmuch as this has never been accomplished, we may suppose that there is a day remaining in which it will be accomplished."[13]

Will there be a restoration of the miraculous gifts at this time?

JE: No, "I don't expect a restoration of these miraculous gifts in the approaching glorious times of the church, nor do I desire it.... It does not appear to me that there is any need of those extraordinary gifts, to introduce this happy state, and set up the kingdom of God through the world: I have seen so much of the power of God in a more excellent way, as to convince me that God can easily do it without [them]."[14]

But as we view things right now, it doesn't look so much like the church is triumphing.

JE: "I would observe that the increase of gospel light and carrying on the work of redemption as it respects the elect church in general, from the first erecting of the church to the end of the world, is very much after the same manner as the carrying on of the same work and the same light in a particular soul from the time of its conversion till it is perfected and crowned in glory." To be sure, there are "ups and downs," and "sometimes the light shines brighter and sometimes it is a dark time.... But in the general grace is growing from its first infusion till it is perfected in glory."[15]

How will this latter day glory of the church be brought about?

JE: "This is a work that will be accomplished by means, by the preaching of the gospel, and the use of the ordinary means of grace, and so shall be gradually brought to pass."[16] "The apostolic age, or the age in which the apostles lived and preached the gospel, was an age of the greatest outpouring of the Spirit of God that ever was." But "we have reason from Scripture prophecy to suppose, that at the commencement of that last and greatest outpouring of the Spirit of God, that is to be in the latter ages of the world, the manner of the work will be very extraordinary, and such as never has yet been seen."[17]

Before the millennium, "the gospel shall be preached to every tongue and kindred and [nation and people]." This will be "before [the] fall of Antichrist." "Heresies and infidelity and superstition among those that have been brought under the light of the gospel will then be abolished," along with an "end to Socinianism and Arianism and Quakerism and Arminianism [and Deism]." And "that other great kingdom of Satan," which is Islam, "shall be utterly overthrown." Then will be seen the "national conversion of the Jews."[18]

How can the individual Christian, or groups of Christians, promote this work best?

JE: "There is no way that Christians in private capacity can do so much to promote the work of God, and advance the kingdom of Christ, as by prayer."[19] "In the text [of Zechariah 8:20-22] we have an account how this future glorious advancement of the church of God should be brought on, or introduced, *viz.*, by great multitudes in different towns and countries taking up a joint resolution, and coming into an express and visible agreement, that they will, by united and extraordinary prayer, seek to God that He would come and manifest Himself, and grant the tokens and fruits of His gracious presence."[20]

Do you believe, in accordance with Revelation 20, that this time of the latter day glory of the church will be followed by a brief time of apostasy and persecution of genuine Christians; and then the second coming of Christ?

JE: This is my belief. "Christ, at His first coming, came to bear the sins of His people for the procuring of their salvation. At His second coming," after the latter day glory of the church, "He will appear without bearing any sins for the bestowment of salvation."[21] And "it is probable that many of the saints at that time will be found suffering persecution, for there are several things in Scripture that seem to hold forth that the time when Christ is coming shall be a time when wickedness shall exceedingly abound and the saints be greatly persecuted."[22]

---

[1] Edwards, *Works* (Yale), 9:461.
[2] Edwards, *Miscellany* 26.
[3] Edwards, *Sermon* on Isaiah 62:4-5.
[4] Edwards, *Sermon* on 2 Corinthians 5:8.
[5] Edwards, *Works*, I:610.
[6] Edwards, *Works* (Yale), 4:358-359.
[7] Edwards, *Miscellany* 740.
[8] Edwards, *Works* (Yale), 5:343.
[9] Edwards, *Miscellany* 911.
[10] Edwards, *Works* (Yale), 5:330-331, 337.
[11] Edwards, *Works* (Yale), 5:446.
[12] Edwards, *Works*, I:607.
[13] Edwards, *Works* (Yale), 18:366.
[14] Edwards, *Works* (Yale), 4:281-282.
[15] Edwards, *Works* (Yale), 9:144-145.
[16] Edwards, *Works* (Yale), 9:459.
[17] Edwards, *Works* (Yale), 4:226, 230.
[18] Edwards, *Works* (Yale), 9:261, 267, 269.
[19] Edwards, *Works* (Yale), 4:518.
[20] Edwards, *Works* (Yale), 5:314.
[21] Edwards, *Sermon* on Hebrews 9:28.
[22] Edwards, *Sermon* on John 1:10.

CHAPTER 12
Edwards on Heaven and Hell

Heaven

When we come to a study of heaven, we are dealing with the doctrine of glorification, which is the final stage of the ordo salutis.

JE: "Christ has brought it to pass, that those whom the Father has given Him should be brought into the household of God; that He and His Father, and His people, should be as one society, one family, that the church should be as it were admitted into the society of the blessed Trinity."[1]

What is heaven going to be like?

JE: "We have but a very imperfect knowledge of the future state of blessedness and of their [the heavenly hosts] employment; without a doubt they have various employments there. We cannot reasonably question but they are employed in contributing to each other's delight. They shall dwell together in society. They shall also probably be employed in contemplating God, His glorious perfections and glorious works, and so gaining knowledge in these things. And doubtless they will be employed in many ways that we know nothing of; but this we may determine: that much of their employment consists in praising God."[2] This we know, that "heaven is a world of love."[3] And we know that "the happiness of the saints in heaven consists partly in that they serve God."[4] Among other things "they shall employ themselves in singing God's praise, or expressing their thoughts to God and Christ, and also to one another; and in going from one part of heaven to another, to behold the glories of God shining in the various parts of it."[5]

You seem to believe that glorification comes in two stages. The first stage begins at the death of the individual Christian, when he enters into the disembodied, intermediate state; the second stage occurs at the time of the final resurrection of the dead.

JE: This is the case.[6]

When does stage one begin?

JE: It begins with the death of the saint, when he is ushered into the presence of God, in Christ: "Death is not only no death for them [the saints], but is a translation to a more glorious life, and is turned into a kind of resurrection from the dead. Death is a happy change to them, and a change that is by far more like a resurrection than a death. It is a change from a state of much sin, and sorrow, and darkness, to a state of perfect light, and holiness, and joy. When a saint dies, he awakes, as it were, out of sleep. This life is a dull, lifeless state; there is but a little spiritual life, and a great deal of deadness; there is but a little light, and a great deal of darkness; there is but a little sense, and a great deal of stupidity and senselessness. But when a godly man dies, all this deadness, and darkness, and stupidity, and senselessness are gone forever, and he enters immediately into a state of perfect life, and perfect light, and activity, and joyfulness."[7]

How does one describe the glory of heaven?

JE: "There is nothing upon earth that will suffice to represent to us the glory of heaven."[8] There "the saints shall have great delight in the society and enjoyment of one another.... The saints in heaven shall all be one society, they shall be united together without any schism, there shall be sweet harmony, and a perfect union."[9] But the *summum bonum* of glorification is that "the saints in heaven will see God. They shall not only see that glorious city [the heavenly Jerusalem], and the saints there, and the holy angels, and the glorified Christ; but they shall see God Himself…with the eye of the soul."[10]

You speak often about the "beatific vision" that the saints will have in heaven. Would you describe this?

JE: A good man "loves God above all else for His own beauty." In heaven, the "good man" sees God "face to face." This is the "beatific vision," which surpasses all other blessings that the saints will have in their final, heavenly state.[11] Here on this earth there are times when God gives His people "views" of His "beauty and excellency." And these "are more precious to [them] than all the treasures of the wicked."[12] But in the heavenly kingdom the saints will see God. This beatific vision consists mainly in a view of the glorified Jesus Christ, the second person of the Godhead: "That beatific vision that the saints will have of God in heaven is in beholding the manifestations that He makes of Himself in the work of redemption. For that arguing of the being and perfection of God that may be *a priori* does not seem to be called seeing God in Scripture, but only that which is by manifestations God makes of Himself in His Son. All other ways of knowing God are by seeing Him in Christ the Redeemer, the image of the invisible God, and in His works; or, the effects of His perfections in His redemption and the fruits of it (which effects are the principal manifestation or shining forth of His perfections). And in conversing with them by Christ which conversation is chiefly about those things done and manifested in this work, if we may judge by the subject of God's conversation with His church by His Word in this world. And so we may infer that business and employment of the saints so far as it consists in contemplation, praise, and conversation is mainly in contemplating the wonders of this work, in praising God for the displays of His glory and love therein, and in conversing about things appertaining to it."[13]

And how is this beatific vision brought about?

JE: By the Holy Spirit. "As it is by the Holy Spirit that a spiritual sight of God is given in this world, so it is the same Holy Spirit by whom the beatific vision is given of God in heaven."[14]

Will the saints in heaven grieve over the lost?

JE: Not at all. "When the saints in glory see the wrath of God executed on ungodly men, it will be no occasion of grief to them, but of rejoicing."[15]

When does the second stage of glorification begin?

JE: At the time of the final resurrection: "As the wicked have not their full punishment until after the resurrection, so neither have the saints their complete happiness. Though they have attained to such exceeding glory, yet they are not yet arrived at its highest degrees, for that is reserved for their final state. The reward which the saints receive after the resurrection, is often spoken of as their chief reward.... So the happiness, that they shall be given at Christ's second coming, is spoken of as the principal happiness."[16]

You have taught that it is natural for us to want to be embodied.

JE: Yes, the non-corporeal state, in this sense, is unnatural: "Redemption is not complete till the resurrection.... So long as the separation between soul and body remains, one of those evils remains that is a part of the penalty of the law.... To be without a body is in itself an evil, because it is a want of that which the soul of man naturally inclines to and desires."[17]

What will the bodies of Christians be like at the resurrection?

JE: The bodies of Christians will be raised both "in an exceeding strength" and "in a wonderful beauty," "for we are told that their bodies shall be like to Christ's glorious body."[18] They will be the same bodies as they had on earth, but glorified. "For the body shall not only return to life, but to a much more glorious state than it was in before dissolution, yea, a much more glorious state than the body of man was in before the Fall."[19]

Doesn't the Scripture say that the saints will reign with Christ, and be blessed by Him?

JE: It does. These same resurrected and glorified saints "shall sit on thrones with Christ, to judge wicked men and angels." And "Christ shall pronounce the blessed sentence upon them [the elect]: 'Come, you blessed of My Father, inherit the kingdom prepared for you from the foundation of the world.'"[20]

Are there degrees of blessedness in heaven?

JE: Yes, there are. "The saints are like so many vessels of different sizes cast into a sea of happiness where every vessel is full.... But after all it is left to God's sovereign pleasure, it is His prerogative to determine the largeness of the vessel."[21] And "the happiness of the saints shall never have any interruption." And the degree of blessedness of the saints "will be according to the degree of their holiness and good works."[22]

It is also certain, is it not, that there will be continual growth in purity, with no sin or corruption to interfere in any way?

JE: "It is certain that the inhabitants of heaven do increase in their knowledge."[23] And "there shall never be any end to their [the saints] glory and blessedness. Therefore it is so often called eternal life, and everlasting life.... The pleasures which there are at God's right hand, are said to be for ever more (Psalm 16:11)." "As God is eternal, so their happiness is eternal; as long as the fountain lasts, they need not fear but they shall be supplied."[24] God's "saints will be progressive in knowledge and happiness to all eternity."[25]

And at this time, when the body of Christ's church is perfect and complete, will be the marriage supper of the Lamb.

JE: Yes, and this day will be glorious, not only for the church, but for Christ as well: "It will be the day of the gladness of Christ's heart; [and] the feast, and pomp, and holy mirth, and joy in this marriage day, will be continued to all eternity.... Then will Christ present His church to His Father...and God shall be all in all; and the glory of God [the Father] and the glory of His Son shall be displayed in heaven in a more abundant manner than ever before."[26]

You are of the opinion that the "new heavens and new earth" will be brand new.

JE: Yes, I am. "The remedy that is promised in Christ is a new heaven and a new earth, a new and much better habitation and state of things, instead of it.... This restoration is equivalent to a resurrection of heaven and earth, and is more than a mere restoration: for it shall be a far more glorious state of things, not only than is immediately before the dissolution or conflagration [of the old world], but more glorious than the state of the world was before the Fall, as the resurrection of the bodies of the saints is more than a mere restitution.... Hence, this new state of things is called a new heaven and a new earth. Christ came to restore all things with respect to the elect that, whatever there is of the ruinous effects of the Fall through the whole universe, all might be fully and perfectly healed in Christ; that old things might pass away and all things become new; that man himself might be a new creature, both in his soul in conversion and sanctification, and in his body by the resurrection, and the world as to him might become a new creation; and so not only himself created anew in Christ Jesus, but everything created anew as to Him fully and perfectly. Revelation 21:5: 'Behold, I make all things new.'"[27]

Hell

Finally, we will discuss the doctrine of hell. You are mindful of the words of Dante, posted over the doors of hell: "Abandon hope all who enter here." I assume you agree with him?

JE: Indeed, I do.

In the doctrine of hell we see the judgment of God most fully.

JE: Yes. In this, God's final judgment on sin, we see "the world of men is to be destroyed, and therefore elect men are taken out of it and carried into the world of angels, and reprobate men left in it to perish and sink with it."[28] And on the great day of judgment, "this lower world, that is to be the place of those that perish, shall be destroyed by fire." "All the visible universe shall be turned into a great furnace."[29]

It seems by this statement that the locus of hell will be the earth; is this correct?

JE: "It is probable that this earth after the conflagration shall be the place of the damned."[30] And "the whole world shall [be] a furnace of the fiercest and most raging heat."[31]

Your view is that hell is a very real place.

JE: It is, indeed. "The doctrine is indeed awful and dreadful, yet it is of God."[32] And "it is a dreadful thing, but yet a common thing for persons to go to hell."[33]

How are we ultimately to view this severe judgment of God on the non-believer? We know that it is for His glory, but how are we to view it?

JE: "Those texts that declare that God delights in mercy, but that judgment is His strange work, which plainly show that God loves to show mercy for mercy's sake, but that He executes judgment for the sake of something else. Psalm 136, throughout, whereby it appears that God's works from the beginning of the world to the end, even judgments on the wicked are works of goodness or mercy to His people."[34]

God "has no pleasure in the destruction or calamity of persons or people.... He is a God that delights in mercy, and judgment is His strange work."[35]

Is the fire of hell spiritual or physical?

JE: Both. "The bodies of wicked men as well as their souls will be punished forever in hell."[36]

Hell, then, is forever.

JE: "The Scripture is plain that the great fire will be that in which the wicked will suffer to all eternity."[37]

You are aware, I am sure, that some teach the doctrine of annihilationism, i.e., that the wicked do not suffer forever, but are annihilated after their death. Some proponents of this view believe that nonexistence through annihilation is worse than eternal punishment. How do you respond?

JE: "Without doubt the misery of the least of sinners that are damned is as terrible or more terrible than no existence, and such that those that endure it would choose rather to cease to be, and be in a state of eternal nonexistence."[38]

How do the wicked react in hell?

JE: "There is no love to God in hell. Everyone perfectly hates Him, without restraint, expressing their hatred to Him, blaspheming and cursing Him, and, as it were, spitting venom at Him. And though they all join together in their enmity and opposition to God, yet there is no union among themselves. They agree to nothing but hatred and expressions of hatred. They hate God, and hate Christ, and hate angels and saints in heaven. And not only so, but [they] hate one another."[39]

And what is it that makes hell, hell?

JE: God. "It is the infinite almighty God that shall become the fire of the furnace."[40] "God will be the hell of the one [non-believer] and the heaven of the other [believer]."[41] Those persons in hell are "being perfectly hated by God."[42]

Will there be degrees of torment in hell?

JE: Yes. "The punishment and misery of wicked men in another world will be in proportion to the sin that they are guilty of."[43]

Just how severe will hell be for the wicked?

JE: It will be so severe that "the damned in hell would be ready to give the world if they could to have their sins to have been one less."[44] Further, "hell's torments may increase this way, *viz.* as the damned may have more and more of a sense of eternity after they have endured misery a thousand years, they may have a more dreadful sense of an eternity of misery than they had at first."[45] Indeed, "wicked men shall see others admitted into glory...[and] this will aggravate their grief and woe."[46]

---

[1] Edwards, *Sermon* on Revelation 5:5-6.
[2] Edwards, *Sermon* on Revelation 14:2.
[3] Edwards, *Sermon* on 1 Corinthians 13:8-10.
[4] Edwards, *Sermon* on Revelation 22:3.
[5] Edwards, *Miscellany* 137.
[6] Edwards, *Works*, II:888-905.
[7] Edwards, *Works*, II:891.
[8] Edwards, *Sermon* on Revelation 21:18.
[9] Edwards, *Sermon* on Romans 2:10.
[10] Edwards, *Works*, II:900.
[11] Edwards, *Sermon* on Psalm 27:4.
[12] *Devotions From the Pen of Jonathan Edwards*, compiled by Ralph G. Turnbull and Don Kistler, 37.
[13] Edwards, *Miscellany* 777.
[14] Edwards, *Sermon* on Romans 2:10.
[15] Edwards, *Sermon* on Revelation 18:20.
[16] Edwards, *Works*, II:893-894.
[17] Edwards, *Miscellany* 644.
[18] Edwards, *Works*, II:894-895.
[19] Edwards, *Miscellany* 806.
[20] Edwards, *Works*, II:895-896.

[21] Edwards, *Miscellany* 367.
[22] Edwards, *Miscellany* 671.
[23] Edwards, *Miscellany* 701.
[24] Edwards, *Works*, II:902.
[25] Edwards, *Miscellany* 435.
[26] Edwards, *Works*, II:896.
[27] Edwards, *Miscellany* 806.
[28] Edwards, *Miscellany* 936.
[29] Edwards, *Miscellany* 952.
[30] Edwards, *Miscellany* 275.
[31] Edwards, *Works* (Yale), 9:509.
[32] Cited in John H. Gerstner, *Jonathan Edwards on Heaven and Hell*, 49.
[33] Edwards, *Sermon* on 1 Corinthians 11:32.
[34] Edwards, *Miscellany* 1081.
[35] Edwards, *Sermon* on Jonah 3:10.
[36] Edwards, *Sermon* on Matthew 10:28.
[37] Edwards, *Sermon* on Revelation 21:8.
[38] Edwards, *Miscellany* 418.
[39] Edwards, *Works* (Yale), 8:390-391.
[40] Cited in Gerstner, *Jonathan Edwards on Heaven and Hell*, 53.
[41] Edwards, *Sermon* on 2 Corinthians 4:18.
[42] Edwards, *Miscellany* 592.
[43] Edwards, *Sermon* on Matthew 5:22.
[44] Edwards, *Sermon* on Romans 1:24.
[45] Edwards, *Miscellany* 441.
[46] Cited in Gerstner, *Jonathan Edwards on Heaven and Hell*, 71.

Bibliography

Armstrong, John H., editor. *Reformation and Revival Journal.* Volume 12, Number 3, Summer 2003.

Bogue, Carl W. *Jonathan Edwards and the Covenant of Grace.* Cherry Hill, New Jersey: Mack Publishing Company, 1975.

Brand, David C. *Profile of the Last Puritan: Jonathan Edwards, Self-Love, and the Dawn of the Beatific.* Atlanta, Georgia: Scholars Press, 1991.

Brown, Robert E. *Jonathan Edwards and the Bible.* Indianapolis, Indiana: Indiana University Press, 2002.

Budgen, Victor. *The Charismatics and the Word of God.* Darlington, England: Evangelical Press, 1989.

Cherry, Conrad. *The Theology of Jonathan Edwards: A Reappraisal.* Bloomington and Indianapolis: Indiana University Press, 1990.

Crampton, W. Gary. *Meet Jonathan Edwards.* Morgan, Pennsylvania: Soli Deo Gloria, 2004.

Crisp, Oliver D. *Jonathan Edwards and the Metaphysics of Sin.* Burlington, Vermont: Ashgate Publishing Company, 2005.

Danaher, William J., Jr. "By Sensible Signs Represented: Jonathan Edwards's Sermons on the Lord's Supper," *Pro Ecclesia,* Volume VII, No. 3, 1998.

Danaher, William J., Jr. *The Trinitarian Ethics of Jonathan Edwards.* Columbia, South Carolina: Columbia University Press, 2004.

Daniel, Curt. "The History of Theology and Calvinism." Springfield, Illinois: Good Books, 2003.

Delattre, Roland A. *Beauty and Sensibility in the Thought of Jonathan Edwards.* New Haven, Connecticut: Yale University Press, 1968.

De Prospo, R. C. *Theism in the Discourse of Jonathan Edwards.* London: Associated University Presses, 1985.

Dodds, Elisabeth. *Marriage to a Difficult Man.* Philadelphia, Pennsylvania: Westminster Press, 1971.

Edwards, Jonathan. *A Jonathan Edwards Reader,* edited by John E. Smith, Harry S. Stout, and Kenneth P. Minkema. New Haven, Connecticut: Yale University Press, 1995.

Edwards, Jonathan. *Altogether Lovely*, collected and edited by Don Kistler. Morgan, Pennsylvania: Soli Deo Gloria, 1997.

Edwards, Jonathan. *Charity and Its Fruits*. Edinburgh: Banner of Truth Trust, 1852, 1986.

Edwards, Jonathan. *Devotions From the Pen of Jonathan Edwards*, compiled by Ralph G. Turnbull and Don Kistler. Morgan, Pennsylvania: Soli Deo Gloria Ministries, 2003.

Edwards, Jonathan. *Images or Shadows of Divine Things*, edited by Perry Miller. New Haven, Connecticut: Yale University Press, 1948.

Edwards, Jonathan. *Jonathan Edwards on Knowing Christ*. Edinburgh: Banner of Truth Trust, 1990.

Edwards, Jonathan. *Jonathan Edwards: Representative Selections*, edited by C. H. Faust and T. H. Johnson. New York: Hill and Wang, 1962.

Edwards, Jonathan. *Justification By Faith Alone*, edited by Don Kistler. Morgan, Pennsylvania: Soli Deo Gloria, 2000.

Edwards, Jonathan. *Our Great and Glorious God*, compiled and edited by Don Kistler. Morgan, Pennsylvania: Soli Deo Gloria, 2003.

Edwards, Jonathan. *Pressing Into the Kingdom*, compiled and edited by Don Kistler. Morgan, Pennsylvania: Soli Deo Gloria, 1998.

Edwards, Jonathan. *Standing in Grace*, edited by Don Kistler. Morgan, Pennsylvania: Soli Deo Gloria, 2002.

Edwards, Jonathan. *The Experience That Counts*, prepared by N. R. Needham. London: Grace Publications Trust, 1991.

Edwards, Jonathan. *The Freedom of the Will*. Morgan, Pennsylvania: Soli Deo Gloria, 1996.

Edwards, Jonathan, editor. *The Life and Diary of David Brainerd*. Grand Rapids, Michigan: Baker Book House, 1949, 2002.

Edwards, Jonathan. *The Puritan Pulpit*, compiled and edited by Don Kistler. Morgan, Pennsylvania: Soli Deo Gloria, 2004.

Edwards, Jonathan. *The Salvation of Souls*, edited by Richard A. Bailey and Gregory A. Wills. Wheaton, Illinois: Crossway Books, 2002.

Edwards, Jonathan. *The True Believer*, edited by Don Kistler. Morgan, Pennsylvania: Soli Deo Gloria, 2001.

Edwards, Jonathan. *The Works of Jonathan Edwards*. New Haven, Connecticut: Yale University Press, General editor, John E. Smith, Harry S. Stout [Hereafter, *Works* (Yale)]:

Volume 1: *Freedom of the Will*, edited by Paul Ramsey, 1957.

Volume 2: *Religious Affections*, edited by John E. Smith, 1959.

Volume 3: *Original Sin*, edited by Clyde A. Holbrook, 1970.

Volume 4: *The Great Awakening*, edited by C.C. Goen, 1972.

Volume 5: *Apocalyptic Writings*, edited by Stephen J. Stein, 1977.

Volume 6: *Scientific and Philosophical Writings*, edited by Wallace E. Anderson, 1980.

Volume 7: *The Life of David Brainerd*, edited by Norman Pettit, 1985.

Volume 8: *Ethical Writings*, edited by Paul Ramsey, 1989.

Volume 9: *A History of the Work of Redemption*, edited by John F. Wilson, 1989.

Volume 10: *Sermons and Discourses, 1720-1723*, edited by Wilson H. Kimnach, 1992.

Volume 11: *Typological Writings*, edited by Wallace E. Anderson, Mason I. Lowance, Jr., and David H. Watters, 1993.

Volume 12: *Ecclesiastical Writings*, edited by David D. Hall, 1994.

Volume 13: *The "Miscellanies," a-500*, edited by Thomas A. Schafer, 1994.

Volume 14: *Sermons and Discourses, 1723-1729*, edited by Kenneth P. Minkema, 1997.

Volume 15: *Notes on Scripture*, edited by Stephen J. Stein, 1998.

Volume 16: *Letters and Personal Writings*, edited by George S. Claghorn, 1998.

Volume 17: *Sermons and Discourses, 1730-1733*, edited by Mark Valeri, 1999.

Volume 18: *The "Miscellanies," 501-832*, edited by Ava Chamberlain, 2000.

Volume 19: *Sermons and Discourses, 1734-1738*, edited by M. X. Lesser, 2001.

Volume 20: *The "Miscellanies," 833-1152*, edited by Amy Plantinga Pauw, 2002.

Volume 21: *Writings on the Trinity, Grace, and Faith*, edited by Sang Hyun Lee, 2003.

Volume 22: *Sermons and Discourses, 1739-1742*, edited by Harry S. Stout and Nathan O. Hatch, 2004.

Volume 23: *The "Miscellanies," 1153-1360*, edited by Douglas A. Sweeney, 2004.

Edwards, Jonathan. *The Works of Jonathan Edwards* (Hereafter, *Works*), 2 volumes, edited by Edward Hickman. Edinburgh: Banner of Truth Trust, 1984.

Edwards, Jonathan. *The Works of President Edwards* [Hereafter *Works* (Worcester)], 8 volumes, edited by Samuel Austin. Worcester, Massachusetts: Isaiah Thomas, 1808-1809.

Edwards, Jonathan. *The Wrath of Almighty God*, edited by Don Kistler. Morgan, Pennsylvania: Soli Deo Gloria, 1996.

Edwards, Jonathan. *To All the Saints of God*, compiled and edited by Don Kistler. Morgan, Pennsylvania: Soli Deo Gloria, 2003.

Edwards, Jonathan. *To the Rising Generation*, compiled and edited by Don Kistler. Orlando, Florida: Soli Deo Gloria, 2005.

Edwards, Jonathan. *Treatise on Grace and Other Posthumously Published Writings*, edited by Paul Helm. Cambridge: James Clarke and Co., 1971.

Fiering, Norman. *Jonathan Edwards's Moral Thought and Its British Context*. Chapel Hill, North Carolina: University of North Carolina Press, 1981.

Fiering, Norman. *Moral Philosophy at Seventeenth Century Harvard*. Chapel Hill, North Carolina: University of North Carolina Press, 1981.

Gerstner, Edna. *Jonathan and Sarah: An Uncommon Union*. Morgan, Pennsylvania: Soli Deo Gloria Publications, 1995.

Gerstner, John H. *Heaven & Hell: Jonathan Edwards on the Afterlife*. Grand Rapids, Michigan: Baker Book House, 1980, 1991.

Gerstner, John H. *Jonathan Edwards: A Mini-Theology*. Wheaton, Illinois: Tyndale House Publishers, 1987.

Gerstner, John H. *Jonathan Edwards, Evangelist*. Morgan, Pennsylvania: Soli Deo Gloria, 1995.

Gerstner, John H. *Steps to Salvation*. Philadelphia, Pennsylvania: Westminster Press, 1960.

Gerstner, John H. *The Rational Biblical Theology of Jonathan Edwards*. 3 volumes. Powhatan, Virginia: Berea Publications; Orlando, Florida: Ligonier Ministries, 1991-1993.

Gerstner, John H. *The Theology of Jonathan Edwards: A Study Guide*. Grand Rapids, Michigan: Outreach Inc., 1987.

Gerstner, John H. "The Theology of Jonathan Edwards," a tape series. Grand Rapids, Michigan: Outreach Inc., 1987.

Grosart, Alexander, editor. *Selections From the Unpublished Writings of*

Jonathan Edwards. Ligonier, Pennsylvania: Soli Deo Gloria Publications, 1992.

Gura, Philip F. *Jonathan Edwards: America's Evangelist*. New York, New York: Hill and Wang, 2005.

Hagopian, David G., editor. *The Genesis Debate*. Mission Viejo: California: Crux Press, 2001.

Hart, D. G., Sean Michael Lucas, and Stephen J. Nichols, editors. *The Legacy of Jonathan Edwards*. Grand Rapids, Michigan: Baker Academic, 2003.

Haykin, Michael A. G. *Jonathan Edwards: The Holy Spirit in Revival*. Webster, New York: Evangelical Press, 2005.

Heppe, Heinrich. *Reformed Dogmatics*, edited by Ernst Bizer, translated by G. T. Thompson. London: Wakeman Great Reprints, 2003.

Hodge, Charles. *Systematic Theology*, volumes I-III. Grand Rapids, Michigan: Wm. B. Eerdmans Publishing Company, 1977.

Holbrook, Clyde A. *The Ethics of Jonathan Edwards*. Ann Arbor, Michigan: University of Michigan Press, 1973.

Holmes, Stephen R. *God of Grace and God of Glory: An Account of the Theology of Jonathan Edwards*. Grand Rapids, Michigan: William B. Eerdmans Publishing Company, 2001.

Hosier, Helen K. *Jonathan Edwards: The Great Awakener*. Uhrichsville, Ohio: Barbour Publishing, 1999.

Hulse, Erroll. *Who Are the Puritans? And What Do They Teach?* Darlington, England: Evangelical Press, 2000.

Jenson, Robert W. *America's Theologian*. New York: Oxford University Press, 1988.

Kistler, Don. "The Character of God," a tape series. Morgan, Pennsylvania: Soli Deo Gloria, 2003.

Kistler, Don. "Jonathan Edwards: His Life and Legacy," a tape series. Morgan, Pennsylvania: Soli Deo Gloria, 2003.

Kling, David W. and Douglas A. Sweeney, editors. *Jonathan Edwards at Home and Abroad*. Columbia, South Carolina: University of South Carolina Press, 2003.

Lee, Sang Hyun and Allen C. Guelzo, editors. *Edwards in Our Time: Jonathan Edwards and the Shaping of American Religion*. Grand Rapids, Michigan: Wm. B. Eerdmans Publishing Company, 1999.

Lee, Sang Hyun. *The Philosophical Theology of Jonathan Edwards*. Princeton, New Jersey: Princeton University Press, 1988.

Lee, Sang Hyun, editor. *The Princeton Companion to Jonathan Edwards.* Princeton, New Jersey: Princeton University Press, 2005.

Logan, Samuel T., Jr. "The Doctrine of Justification in the Theology of Jonathan Edwards," *Westminster Theological Journal* 46:1984.

Manspeaker, Nancy. *Jonathan Edwards: A Bibliographical Synopsis.* Lewiston, New York: E. Mellen Press, 1981.

Marsden, George M. *Jonathan Edwards: A Life.* New Haven, Connecticut: Yale University Press, 2003.

Mayhew, George Noel. *The Relation of the Theology of Jonathan Edwards to Contemporary Penological Theory and Practice.* Chicago: University of Chicago Libraries, 1935.

McClymond, Michael J. *Encounters with God: An Approach to the Theology of Jonathan Edwards.* New York: Oxford University Press, 1998.

McDermott, Gerald R. *Jonathan Edwards Confronts the Gods.* New York: Oxford University Press, 2000.

McDermott, Gerald R. *One Holy and Happy Society.* University Park, Pennsylvania: Pennsylvania State University Press, 1992.

McDermott, Gerald R. *Seeing God: Jonathan Edwards and Spiritual Discernment.* Vancouver, Canada: Regent College Publishing, 2000.

McMahon, C. Matthew. *The Two Wills of God: Does God Really Have Two Wills?* New Lenox, Illinois: Puritan Publications, 2005.

Miller, Perry. *Jonathan Edwards.* New York: Meridian, 1959.

Moody, Josh. *Jonathan Edwards and the Enlightenment: Knowing the Presence of God.* Lanham, Maryland: University Press of America, 2005.

Morimoto, Anri. *Jonathan Edwards and the Catholic Vision of Salvation.* University Park, Pennsylvania: Pennsylvania State University Press, 1995.

Morgan, Irvonwy. *The Godly Preachers of the Elizabethan Church.* London: Epworth Press, 1965.

Morris, William S. *The Young Jonathan Edwards.* Eugene, Oregon: Wipf & Stock Publishers, 2005.

Murray, Iain H. *Jonathan Edwards: A New Biography.* Edinburgh: Banner of Truth Trust, 1987.

Nichols, Stephen J. *An Absolute Sort of Certainty: The Holy Spirit and the Apologetics of Jonathan Edwards.* Phillipsburg, New Jersey: Presbyterian and Reformed Publishing Company, 2003.

Nichols, Stephen J. *Jonathan Edwards: A Guided Tour of His Life and Thought.* Phillipsburg, New Jersey: Presbyterian and Reformed Publishing Company, 2001.

Packer, J.I. *A Quest For Godliness.* Wheaton, Illinois: Crossway Books, 1990.

Parrish, Archie, and R. C. Sproul. *The Spirit of Revival: Discovering the Wisdom of Jonathan Edwards.* Wheaton, Illinois: Crossway Books, 2000.

Pauw, Amy Plantinga. *The Supreme Harmony of All: The Trinitarian Theology of Jonathan Edwards.* Grand Rapids, Michigan: Wm. B. Eerdmans Publishing Company, 2002.

Piper, John. *Future Grace.* Sisters, Oregon: Multnomah Press, 1995.

Piper, John. *God's Passion for His Glory.* Wheaton, Illinois: Crossway Books, 1998.

Piper, John. *The Pleasures of God.* Portland, Oregon: Multnomah Press, 1991.

Piper, John. *The Supremacy of God in Preaching.* Grand Rapids, Michigan: Baker Book House, 1990.

Piper, John, and Justin Taylor, editors. *A God Entranced Vision of All Things: The Legacy of Jonathan Edwards.* Wheaton, Illinois: Crossway Books, 2004.

Reymond, Robert L. *A New Systematic Theology of the Christian Faith.* Nashville, Tennessee: Thomas Nelson Publishers, 1998.

Schaff, Philip. *History of the Christian Church.* Vols. I-VIII. Grand Rapids: Michigan: William B. Eerdmans Publishing Company, 1910, 1988.

Scheick, William J. *The Writings of Jonathan Edwards: Theme, Motif, and Style.* College Station, Texas: Texas A & M University Press, 1975.

Simonson, Harold J. *Jonathan Edwards: Theologian of the Heart.* Grand Rapids, Michigan: Wm. B. Eerdmans Publishing Company, 1974.

Smith, Chard Powers. *Yankees and God.* New York: Hermitage House, 1954.

Smith, John E. *Jonathan Edwards: Puritan, Preacher, Philosopher.* Notre Dame, Indiana: Notre Dame Press, 1992.

Sproul, R. C. John H. Gerstner, and Arthur Lindsley. *Classical Apologetics.* Grand Rapids, Michigan: Zondervan Publishing House, 1984.

Stein, Stephen J. editor. *Jonathan Edwards's Writings: Text, Context,*

Interpretation. Bloomington, Indiana: Indiana University Press, 1996.

Steele, David N. and Curtis C. Thomas. *The Five Points of Calvinism.* Phillipsburg, New Jersey: Presbyterian and Reformed Publishing Company, 1963.

Storms, C. Samuel. *Tragedy in Eden: Original Sin in the Theology of Jonathan Edwards.* Lanham, Maryland: University Press of America, 1985.

Townsend, Harvey G. *The Philosophy of Jonathan Edwards.* Eugene, Oregon: The University Press, 1955.

Warfield, Benjamin B. *Studies in Theology.* Edinburgh: Banner of Truth Trust, 1988.

Zakai, Avihu. *Jonathan Edwards's Philosophy of History: The Re-enchantment of the World in the Age of Enlightenment.* Princeton, New Jersey: Princeton University Press, 2003.

Printed in the United States
56802LVS00002B/526-621

9 781892 777768